Bond
No.1 for exam success

AF077801

Non-verbal Reasoning

Assessment Papers

8–9 years

OXFORD
UNIVERSITY PRESS

OXFORD
UNIVERSITY PRESS

Great Clarendon Street, Oxford, OX2 6DP, United Kingdom

Oxford University Press is a department of the University of Oxford. It furthers the University's objective of excellence in research, scholarship, and education by publishing worldwide. Oxford is a registered trade mark of Oxford University Press in the UK and in certain other countries

First published in 2015
This edition published in 2021

British Library Cataloguing in Publication Data
Data available

978-0-19-277995-3

10 9 8 7 6

Paper used in the production of this book is a natural, recyclable product made from wood grown in sustainable forests.
The manufacturing process conforms to the environmental regulations of the country of origin.

Printed in China

Acknowledgements

The publishers would like to thank the following for permissions to use copyright material:

Page make-up: OKS Prepress, India
Illustrations: Nigel Kitching
Cover illustrations: Lo Cole

Although we have made every effort to trace and contact all copyright holders before publication this has not been possible in all cases. If notified, the publisher will rectify any errors or omissions at the earliest opportunity.

Links to third party websites are provided by Oxford in good faith and for information only. Oxford disclaims any responsibility for the materials contained in any third party website referenced in this work.

The manufacturer's authorised representative in the EU for product safety is Oxford University Press España S.A. of El Parque Empresarial San Fernando de Henares, Avenida de Castilla, 2 – 28830 Madrid (www.oup.es/en or product.safety@oup.com). OUP España S.A. also acts as importer into Spain of products made by the manufacturer.

Before you get started

What is Bond?

This book is part of the Bond Assessment Papers series for non-verbal reasoning, which provides a **thorough and continuous course in non-verbal reasoning** from ages six to twelve. It builds up non-verbal reasoning skills from book to book over the course of the series.

What does this book cover?

Non-verbal reasoning questions can be grouped into four distinct groups: identifying shapes, missing shapes, rotating shapes, coded shapes and logic. This book develops an understanding of these groups through practice of seven different question types: finding the odd one out, completing a visual sequence, completing a shape, completing a visual analogy, reflections, hidden shapes and coded shapes. The questions at this level employ a mixture of pictures and pure shapes. From the next book on, the questions will only involve shapes.

The age given on the cover is for guidance only. As the papers are designed to be reasonably challenging for the age group, any one child may naturally find him or herself working above or below the stated age. The important thing is that children are always encouraged by their performance. Working at the right level is the key to this.

What does the book contain?

- **6 papers** – each one contains 48 questions.
- **Scoring devices** – there is a scoring box at the end of each test and a Progress Chart at the back. The chart is a visual and motivating way for children to see how they are doing. Encouraging them to colour in the chart as they go along and to try to beat their last score can be highly effective!
- **Next Steps Planner** – advice on what to do after finishing the papers can be found on the inside back cover.
- **Answers** – located in an easily-removed central pull-out section.

How can you use this book?

One of the great strengths of Bond Assessment Papers is their flexibility. They can be used at home, school and by tutors to:

- provide regular non-verbal reasoning practice in **bite-sized chunks**
- **highlight strengths and weaknesses** in the core skills
- identify **individual needs**
- set **homework**
- set **timed formal practice** tests – allow about 35 minutes.

It is best to start at the beginning and work through the papers in order.

What does a score mean and how can it be improved?

If children colour in the Progress Chart at the back, this will give an idea of how they are doing. The Next Steps Planner inside the back cover will help you to decide what to do next to help a child progress. We suggest that it is always valuable to go over any wrong answers with children.

Don't forget the website . . . !

Visit www.bond11plus.co.uk for lots of advice, information and suggestions on everything to do with Bond, helping children to do their best, and exams.

Paper 1

Which is the odd one out? Circle the letter.

Example

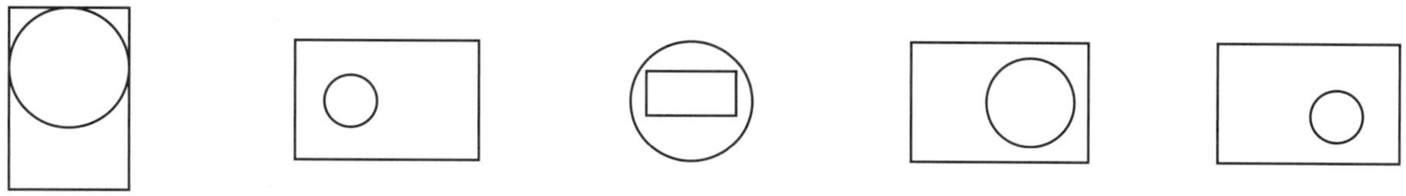

a b (c) d e

1

a b c d e

2

a b c d e

3

a b c d e

4

a b c d e

5

a b c d e

6

a b c d e

7
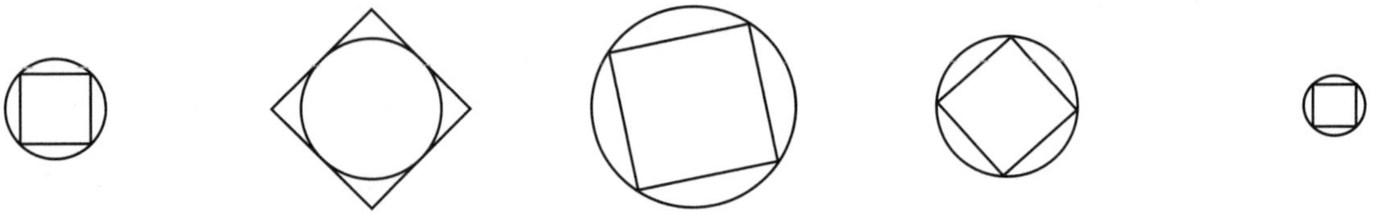
a b c d e

8
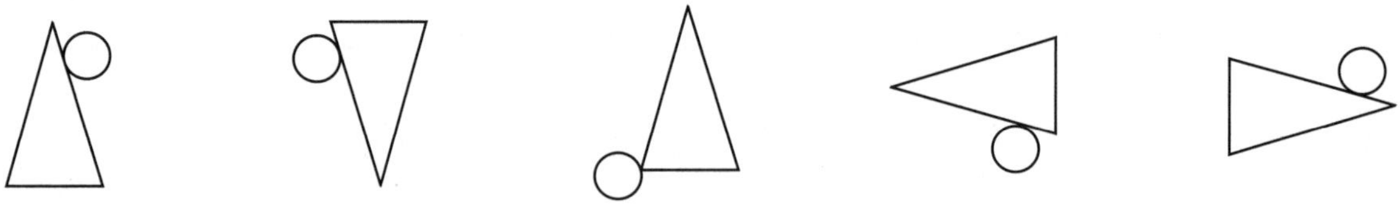
a b c d e

9

a b c d e

10
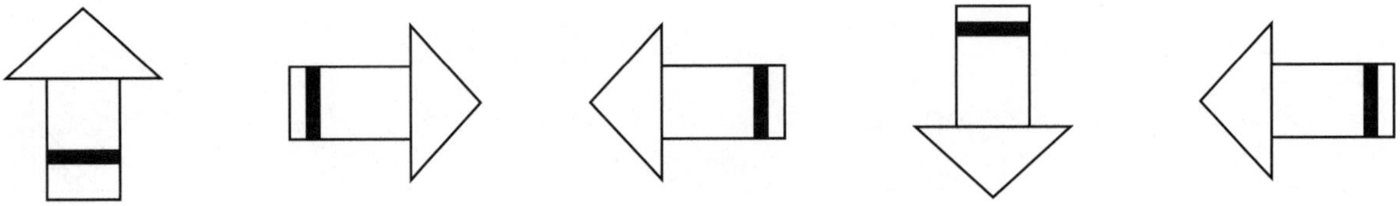
a b c d e

11
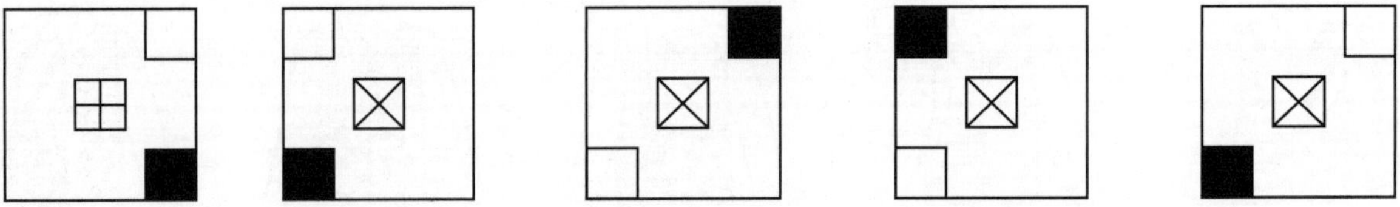
a b c d e

12

a b c d e

Which one comes next? Circle the letter.

Example

?

a b c d e

13

?

a b c d e

14

?

a b c d e

15

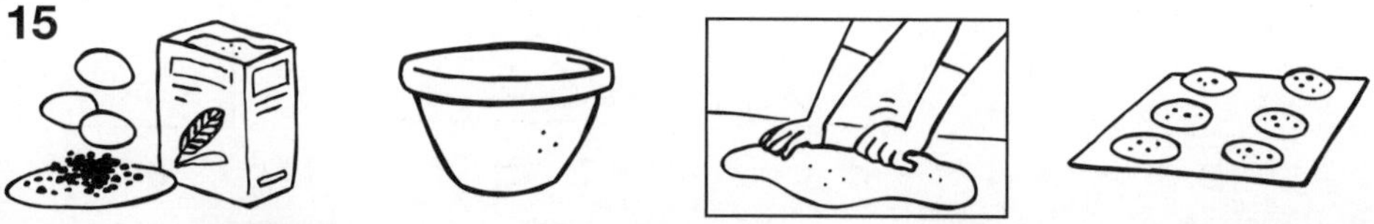

?

a b c d e

16

?

a b c d e

17

?

a b c d e

18

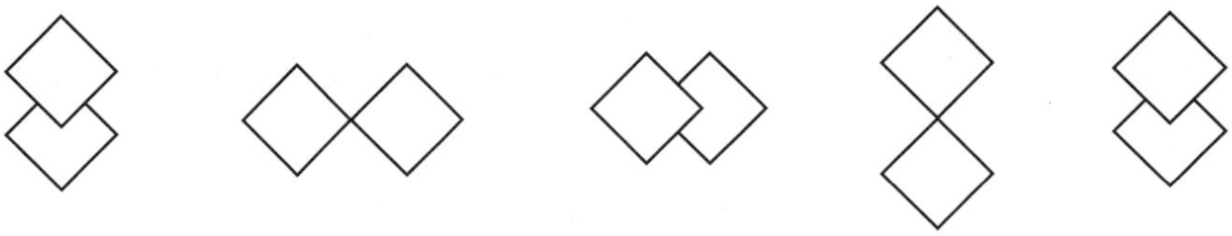

?

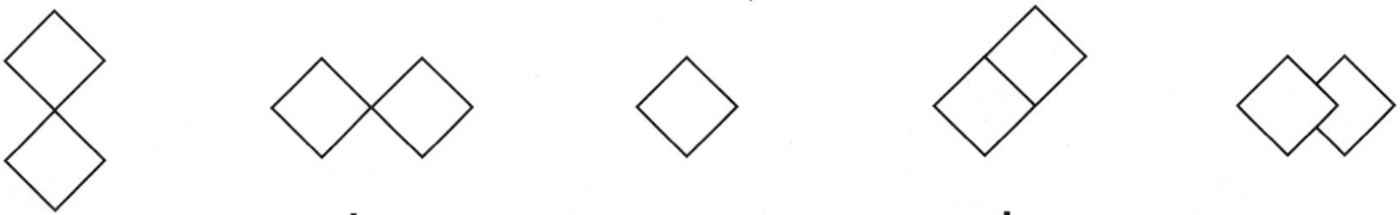

a b c d e

19

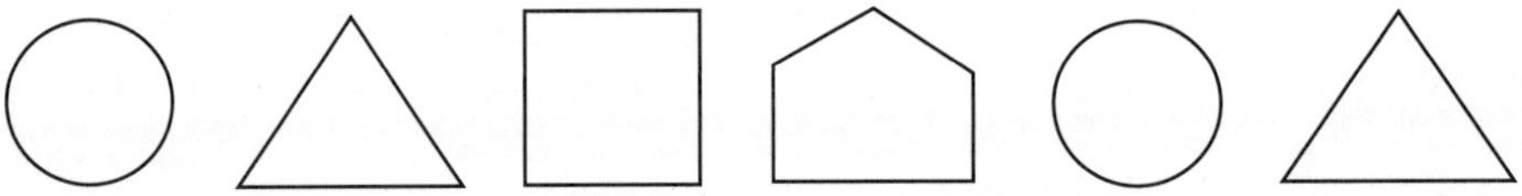

?

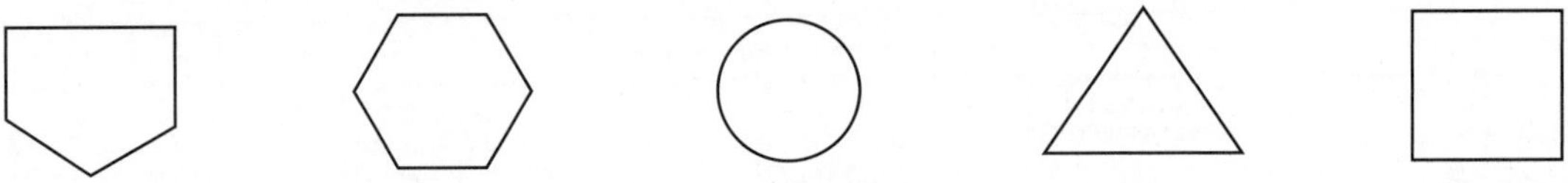

a b c d e

20

× ✓ £ = × ✓ ?

✓	×	£	=	$
a	b	c	d	e

21

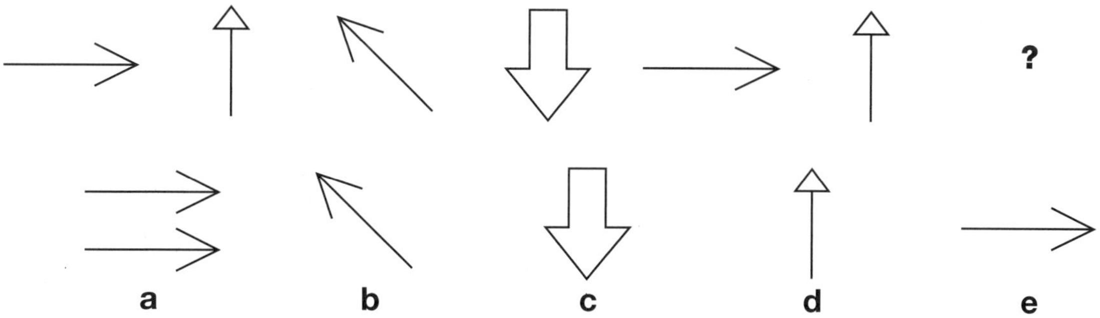

22

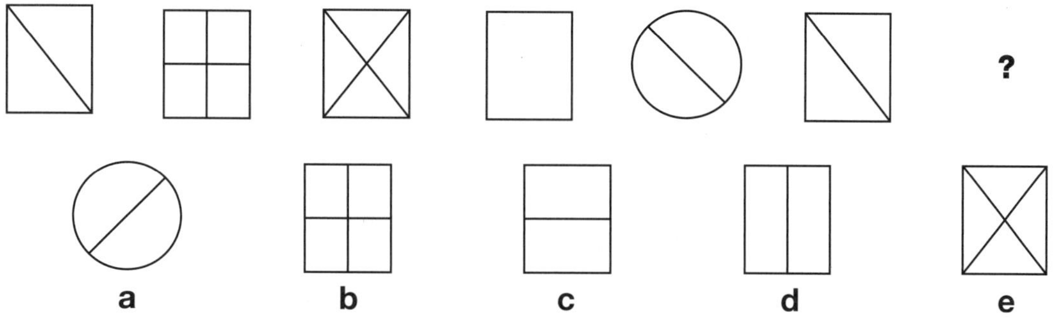

23

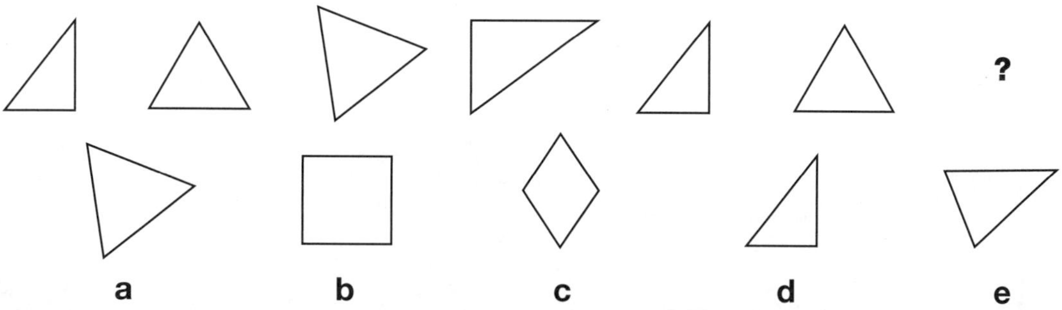

24

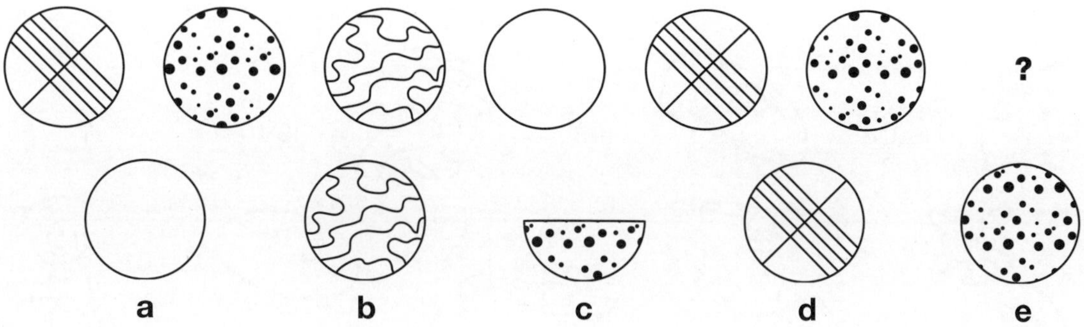

Which picture completes the second pair in the same way as the first pair? Circle the letter.

Example

 is to  as  is to **?**

 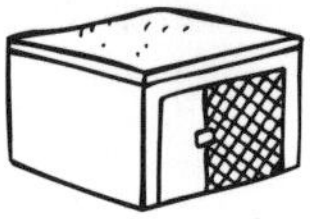 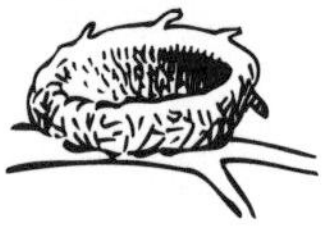  

(a) **b** **c** **d** **e**

25

 is to  as  is to **?**

a **b** **c** **d** **e**

26

 is to  as  is to **?**

a **b** **c** **d** **e**

27

 is to  as 

is to **?**

  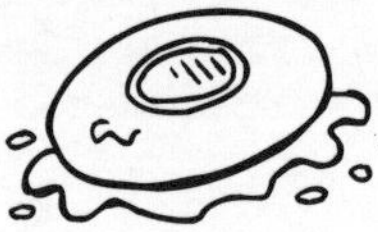 

a **b** **c** **d** **e**

28  is to  as  is to **?**

a **b** **c** **d** **e**

29  is to 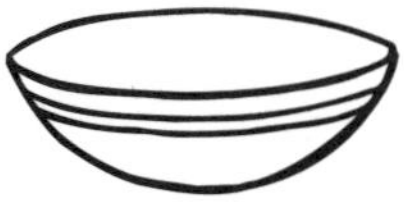 as  is to **?**

a **b** **c** **d** **e**

30  is to  as 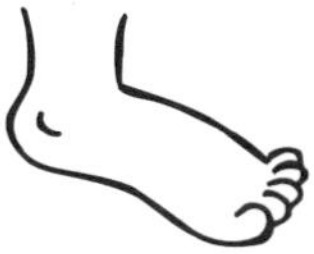 is to **?**

a **b** **c** **d** **e**

31  is to  as  is to **?**

a **b** **c** **d** **e**

32  is to  as  is to **?**

a **b** **c** **d** **e**

33 

is to  as  is to **?**

a

b

c

d

e

34  is to  as  is to **?**

a

b

c

d

e

35  is to  as  is to **?**

a

b

c

d

e

36  is to  as  is to **?**

a

b

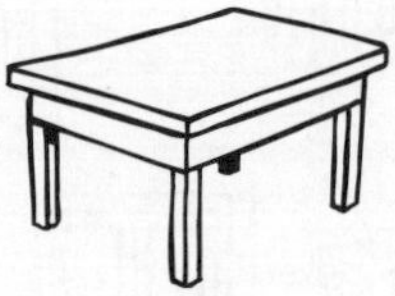
c

d

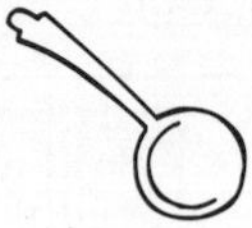
e

In which larger picture is the smaller picture hidden? Circle the letter.

Example

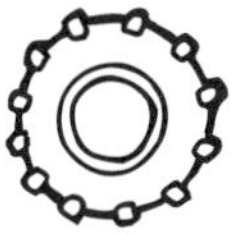

a b c d e

37

a b c d e

38

a b c d e

39

a b c d e

40

a b c d e

41

a b c d e

42

a b c d e

Which shape or picture completes the larger square? Circle the letter.

Example

a b (c) d e

43

a b c d e

44

a b c d e

45

a b c d e

46

a b c d e

47

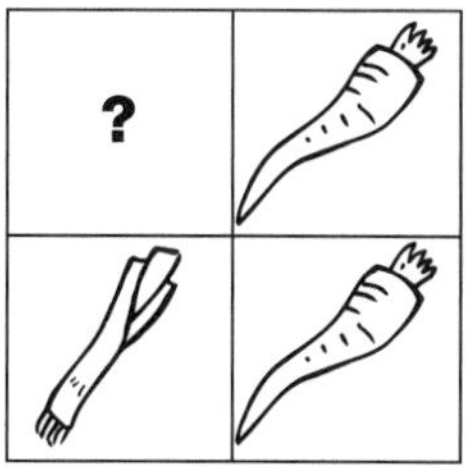

a

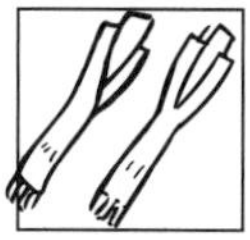

b

c

d

e

48

a

b

c

d

e

Now go to the Progress Chart to record your score! Total ◯ 48

Paper 2

Which is the odd one out? Circle the letter.

Example

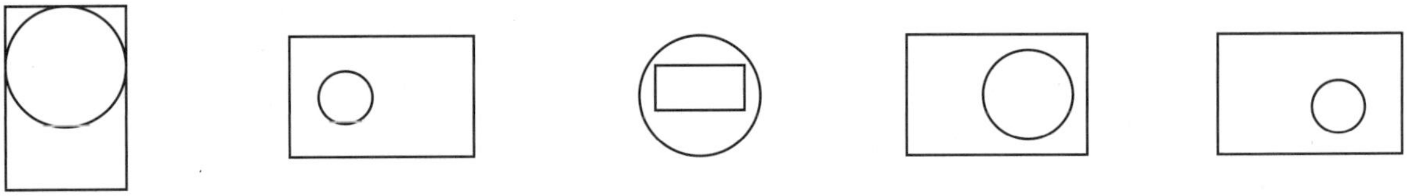

a b (c) d e

1

a b c d e

2

a b c d e

3

a b c d e

4

a b c d e

5

a b c d e

6

a b c d e

7

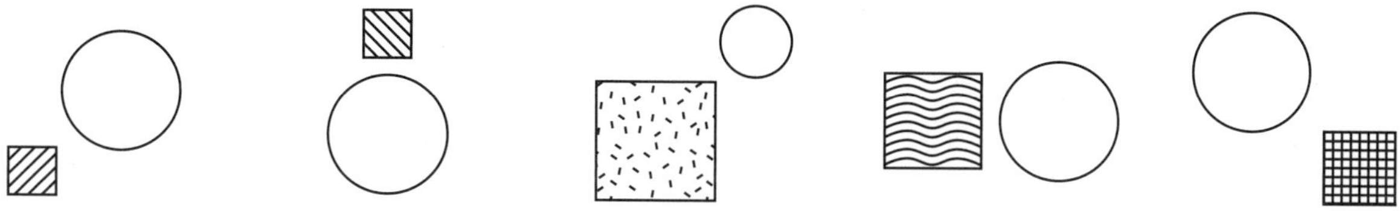

a b c d e

8

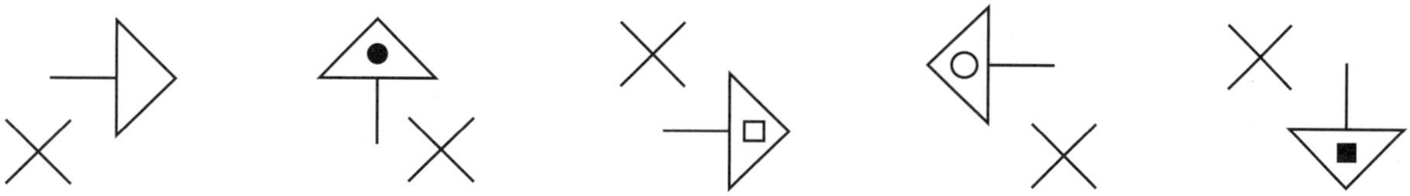

a b c d e

9

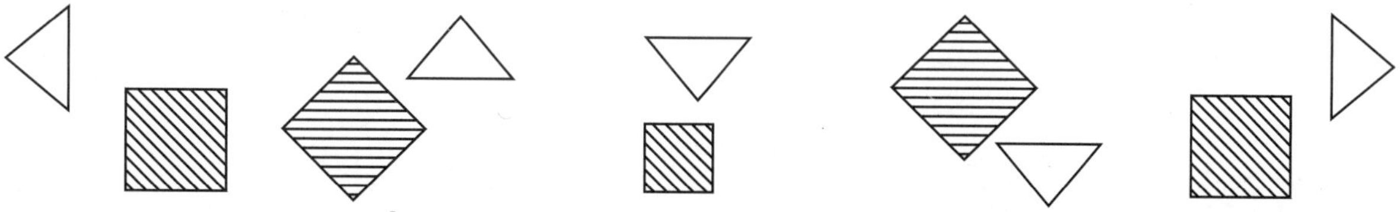

a b c d e

10

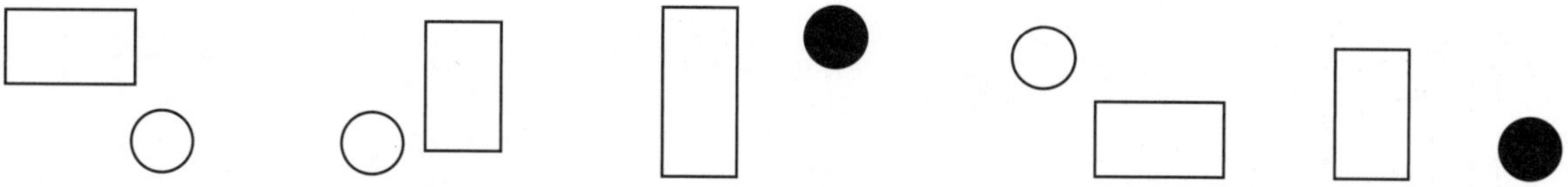

a b c d e

11

a b c d e

12

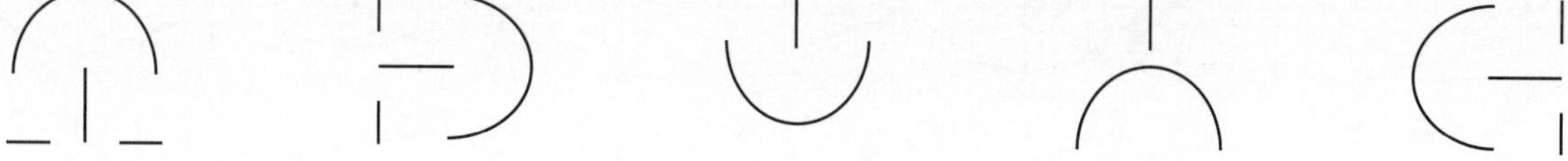

a b c d e

Which one comes next? Circle the letter.

Example

?

a b c d e

13

?

a b c d e

14

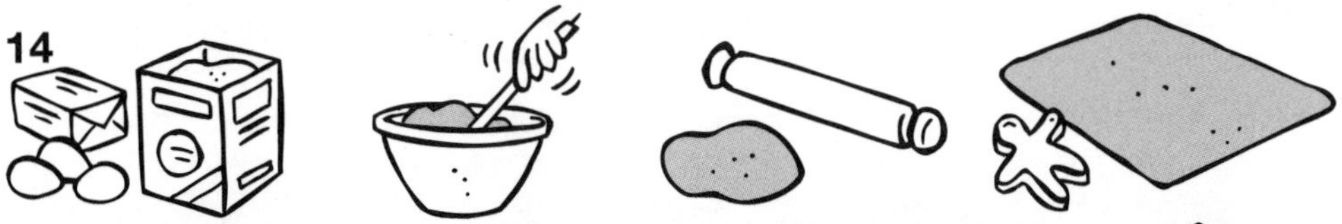

?

a b c d e

15

?

a b c d e

16

?

a b c d e

17

?

a b c d e

18

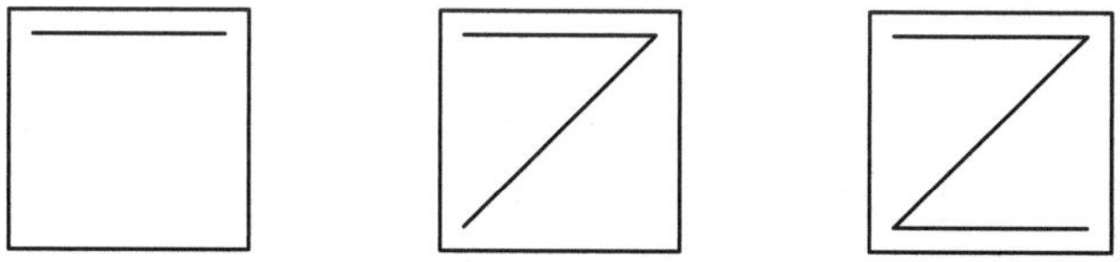

?

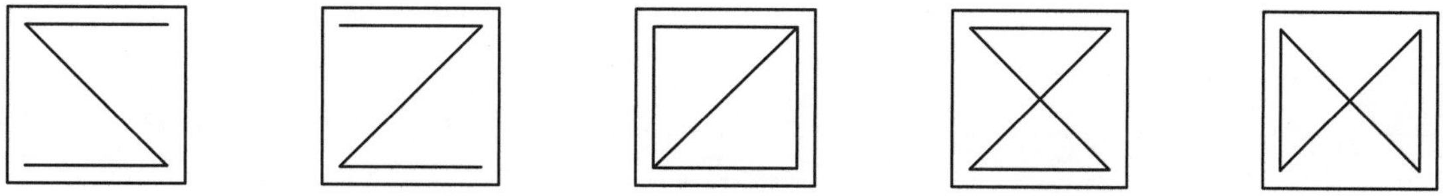

a b c d e

19

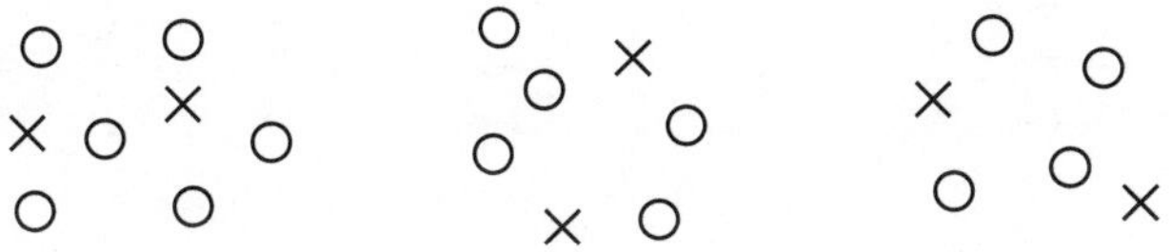

?

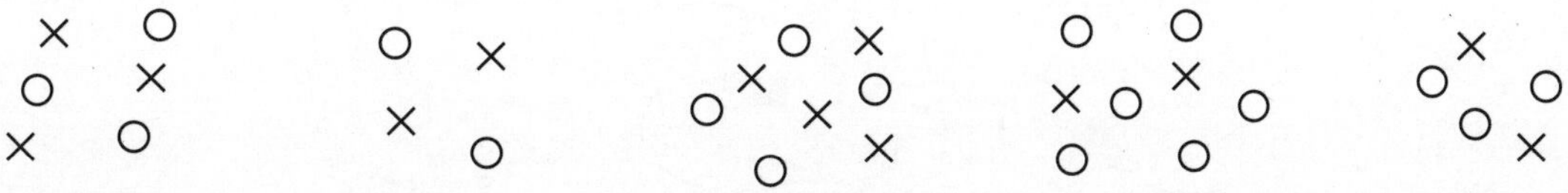

a b c d e

20

a **b** **c** **d** **e**

21

a **b** **c** **d** **e**

22

a **b** **c** **d** **e**

23

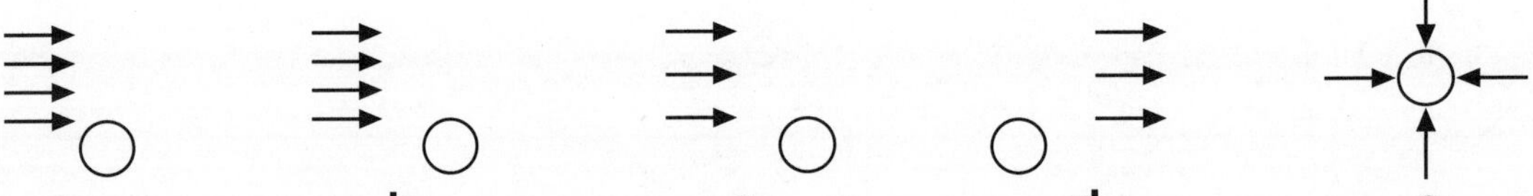

a **b** **c** **d** **e**

24

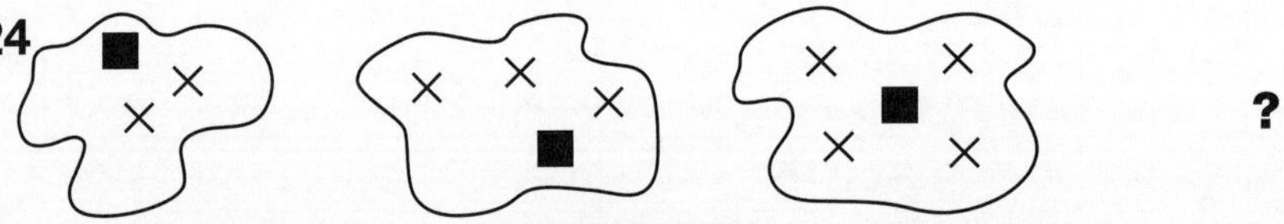

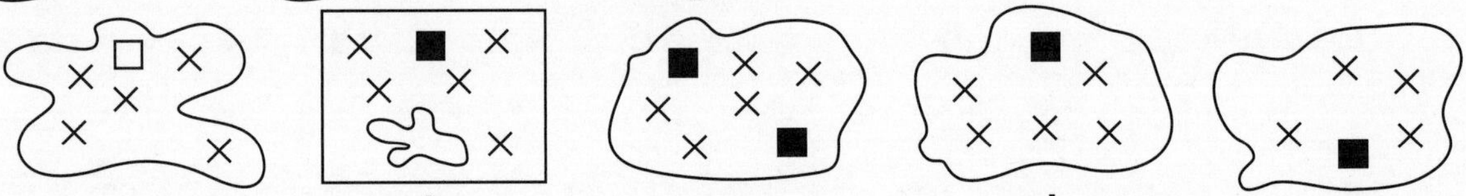

a **b** **c** **d** **e**

Which shape or pattern completes the second pair in the same way as the first pair? Circle the letter.

Example

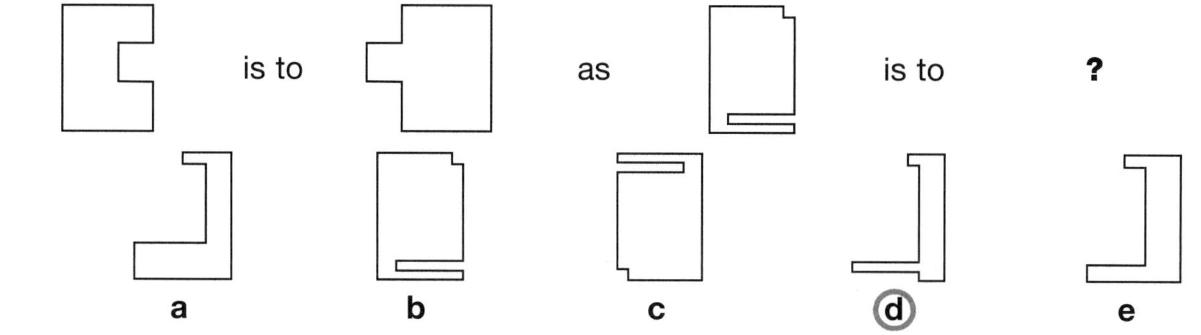

25

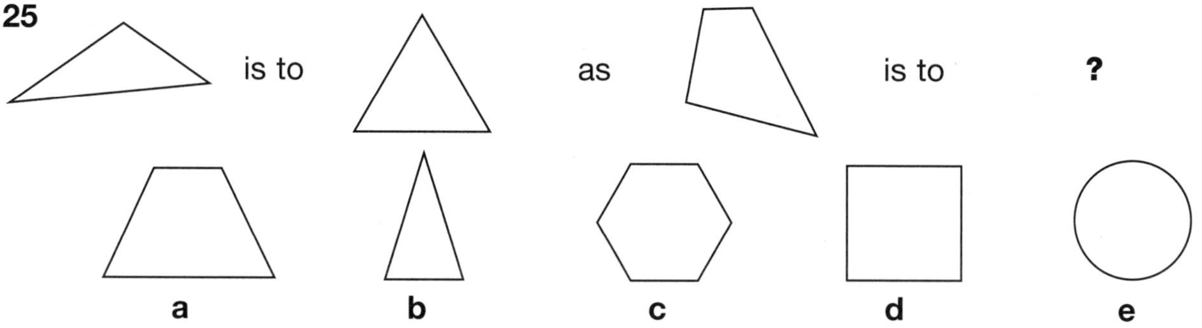

26

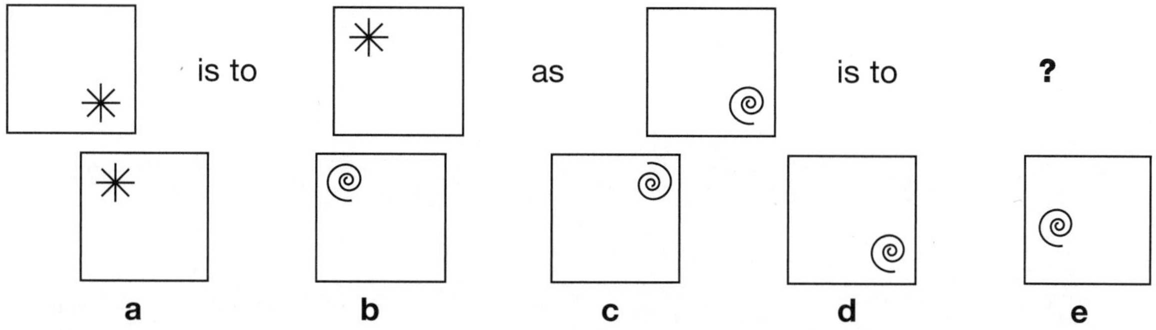

27

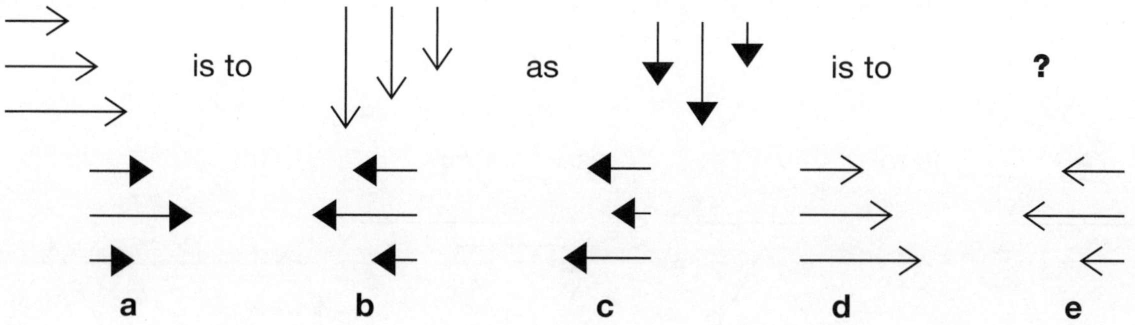

28

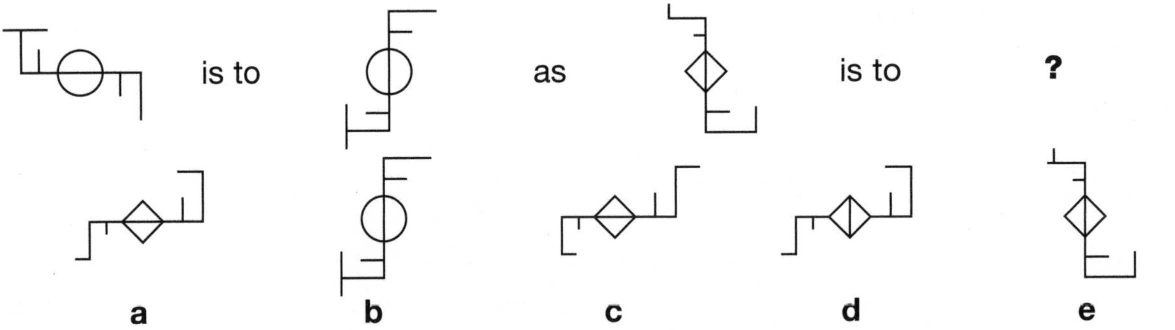
is to
as
is to
?
a
b
c
d
e

29

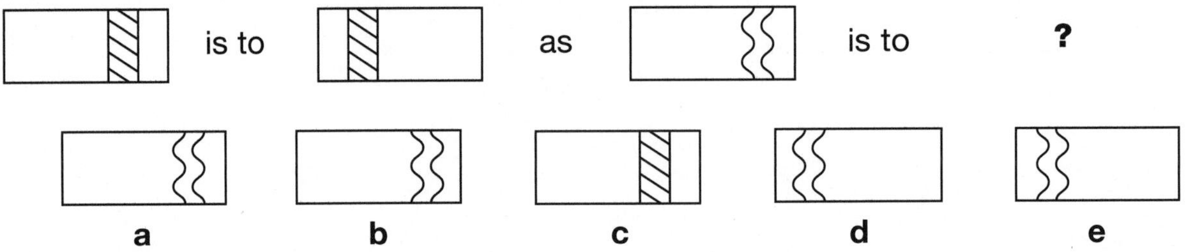
is to
as
is to
?
a
b
c
d
e

30

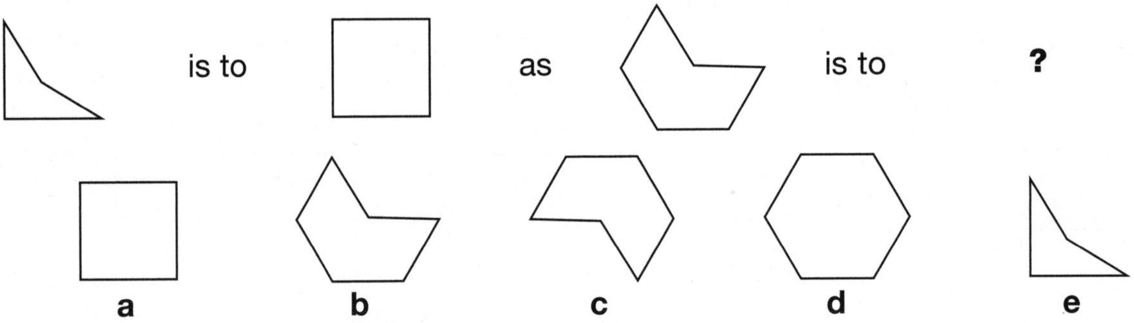
is to
as
is to
?
a
b
c
d
e

31

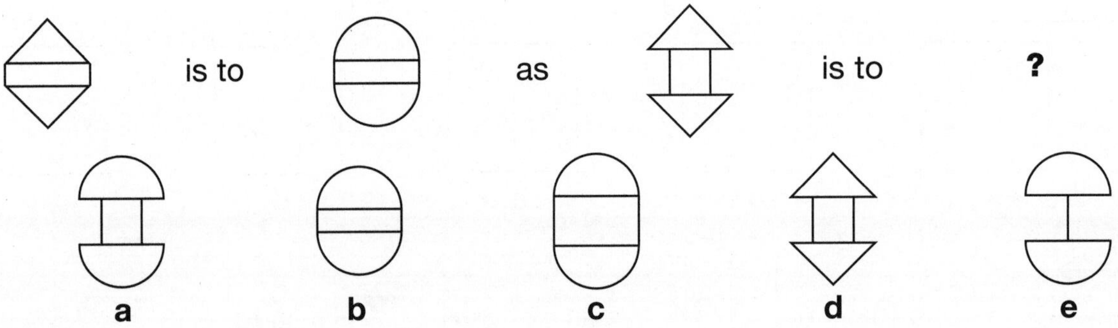
is to
as
is to
?
a
b
c
d
e

32

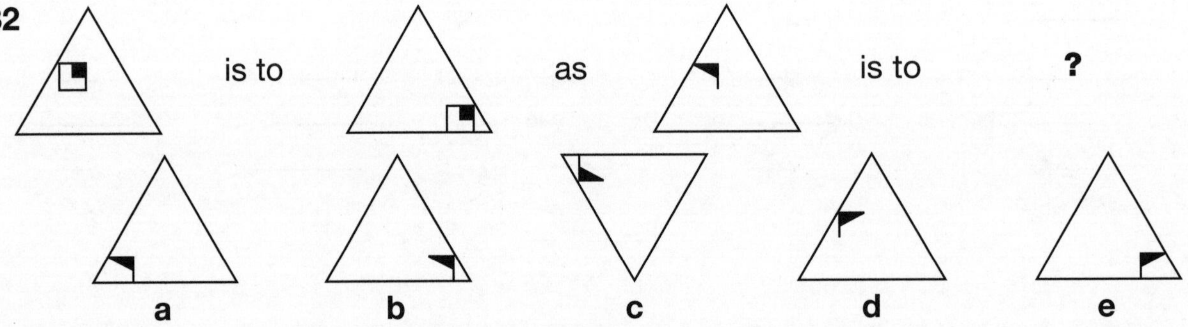
is to
as
is to
?
a
b
c
d
e

33

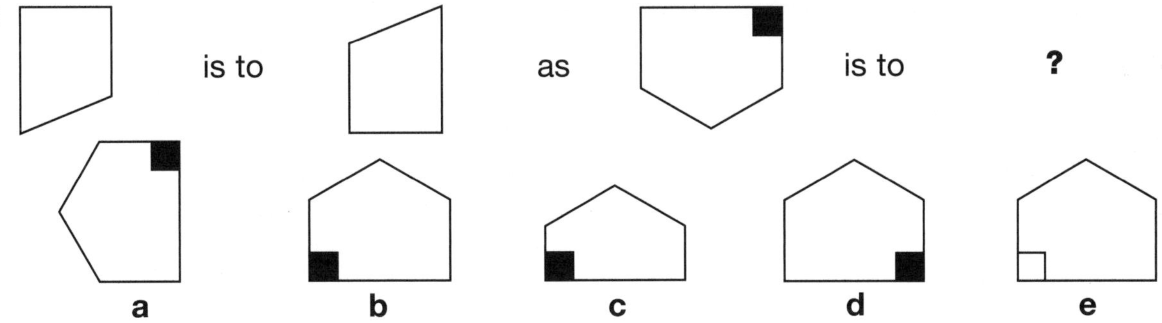
is to
as
is to
?
a
b
c
d
e

34

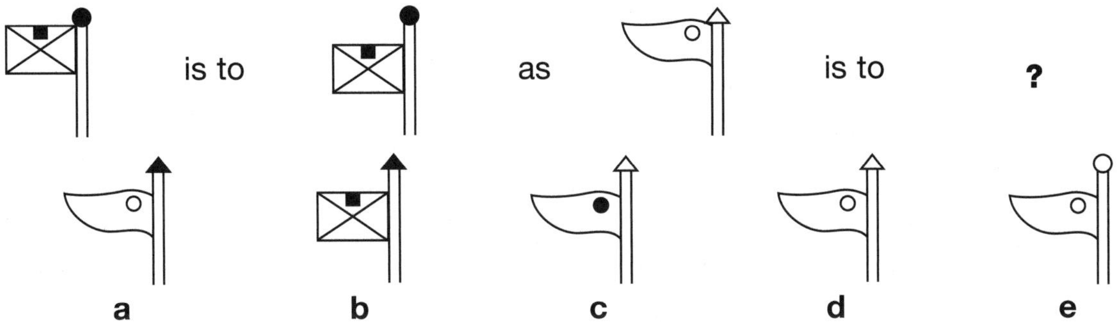
is to
as
is to
?
a
b
c
d
e

35

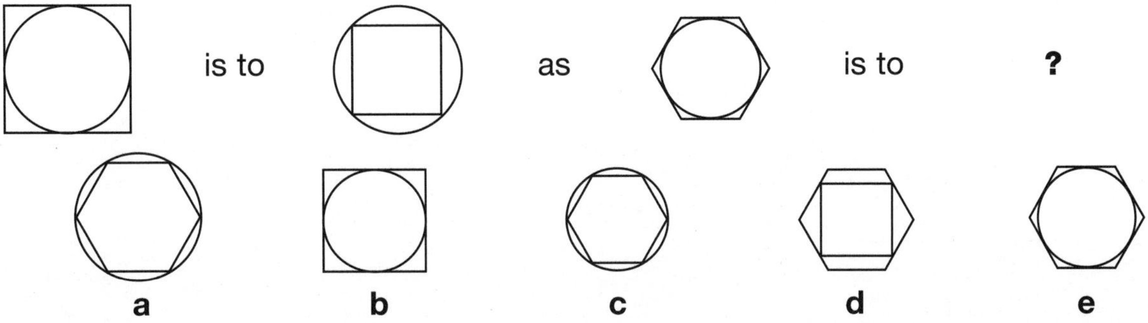
is to
as
is to
?
a
b
c
d
e

36

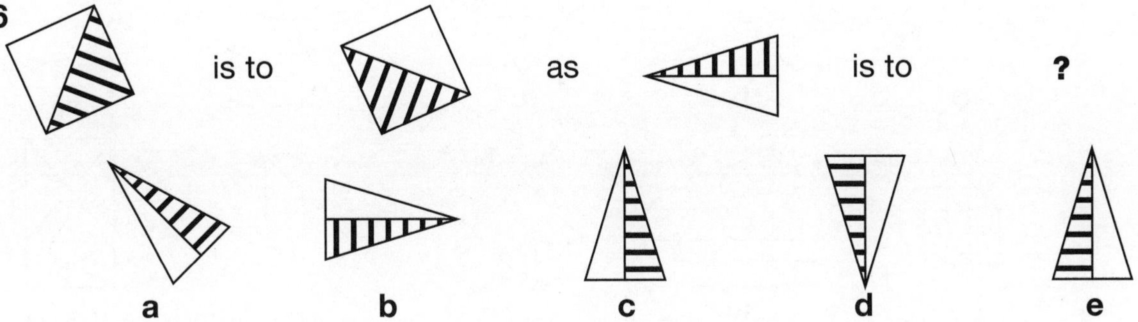
is to
as
is to
?
a
b
c
d
e

In which larger shape is the shape on the left hidden? Circle the letter.

Example

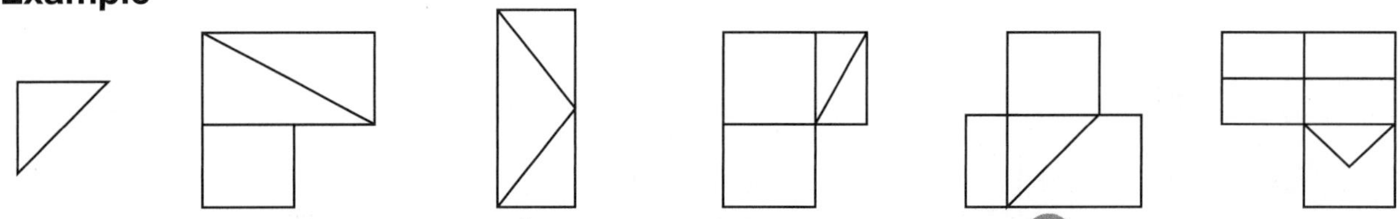

a b c d e

37

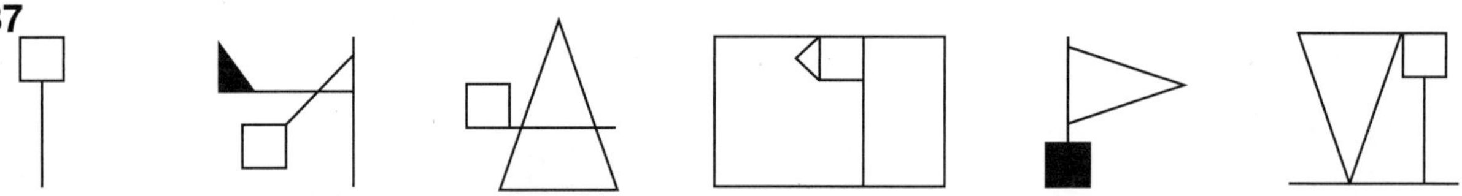

a b c d e

38

a b c d e

39

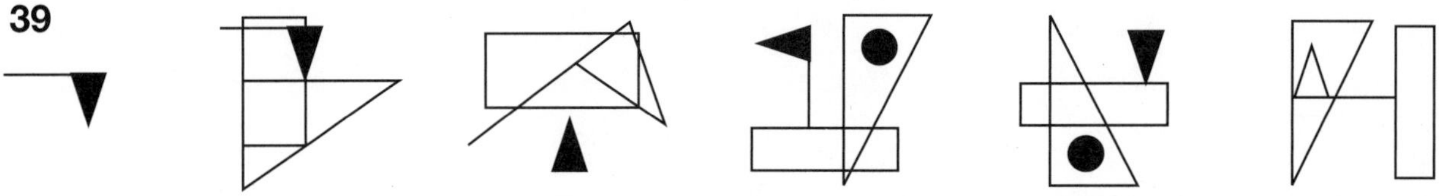

a b c d e

40

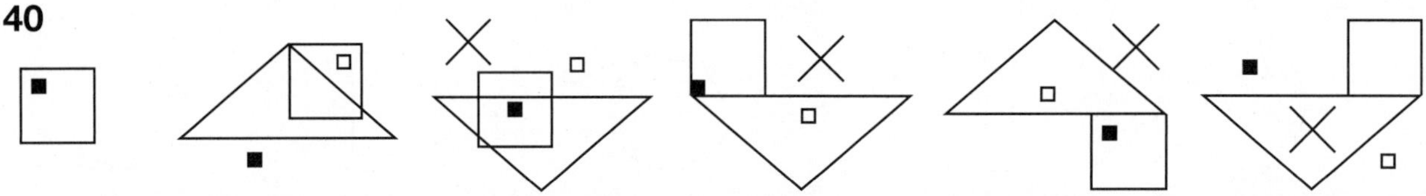

a b c d e

41

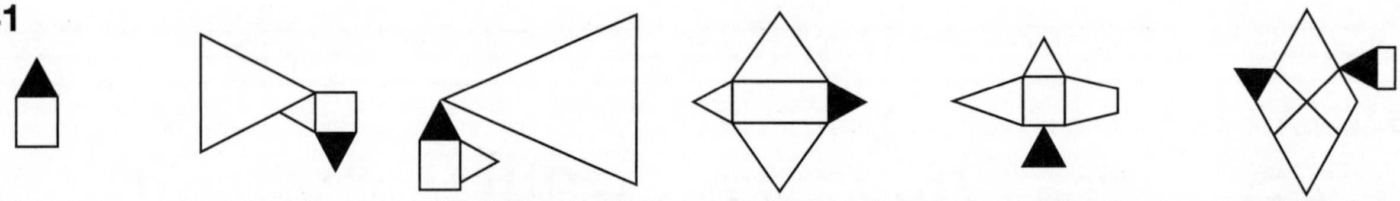

a b c d e

42

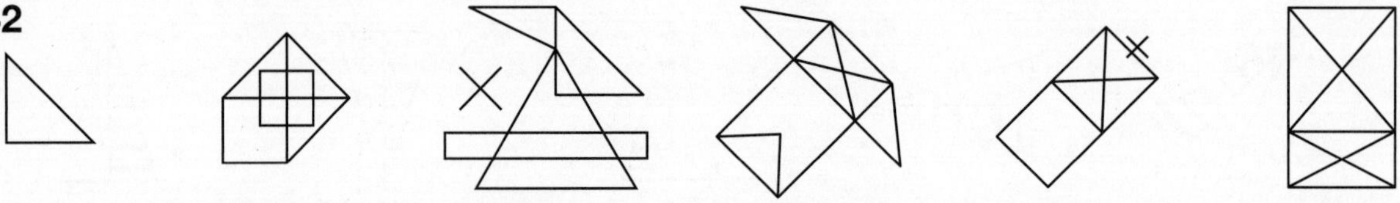

a b c d e

Which picture on the right is the reflection of the picture given on the left, in the dotted mirror line? Circle the letter.

Example

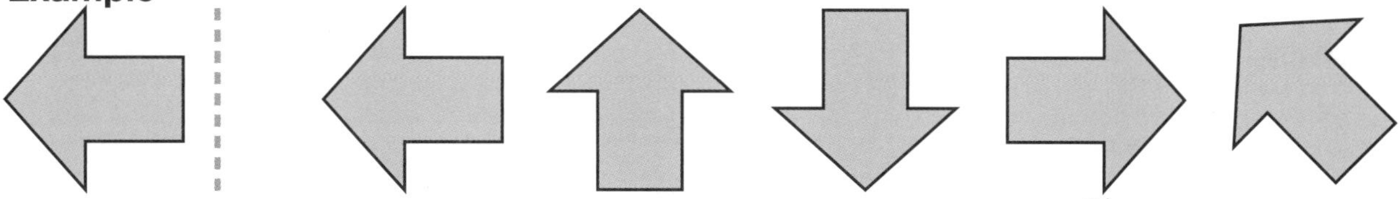

a b c d e

43

a b c d e

44

a b c d e

45

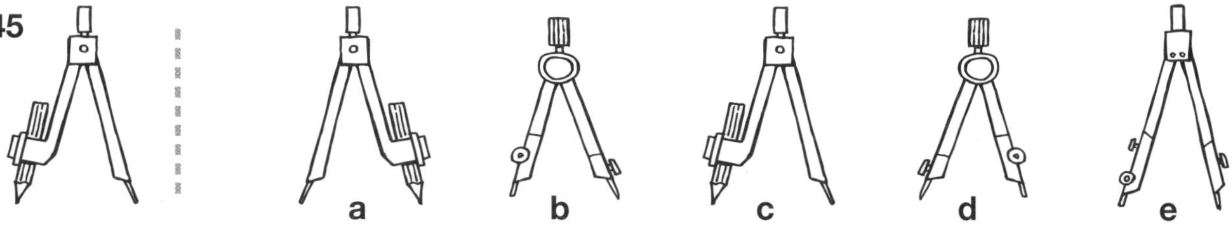

a b c d e

46

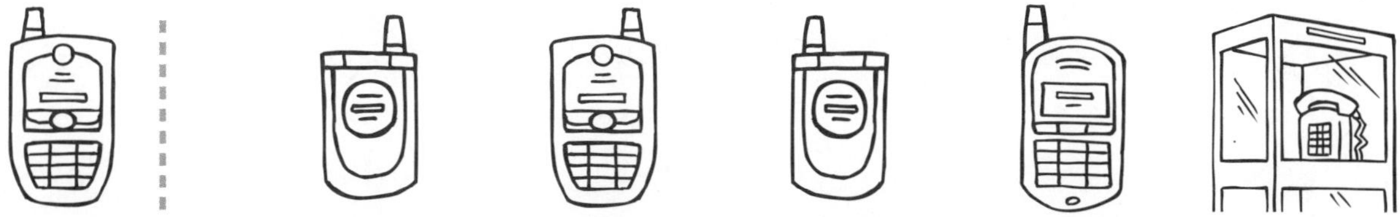

a b c d e

47

a b c d e

48

a b c d e

Paper 3

Which is the odd one out? Circle the letter.

Example

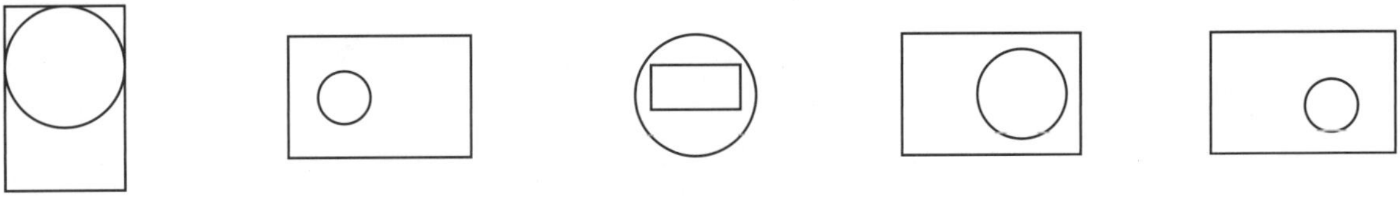

a b (c) d e

1

a b c d e

2

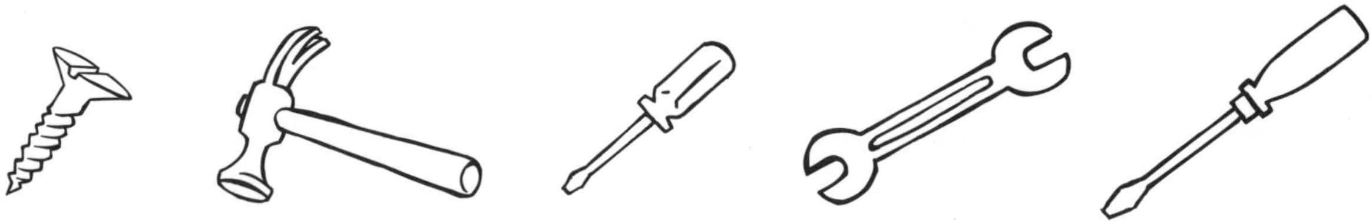

a b c d e

3

a b c d e

4

a b c d e

5

a b c d e

6

a b c d e

7

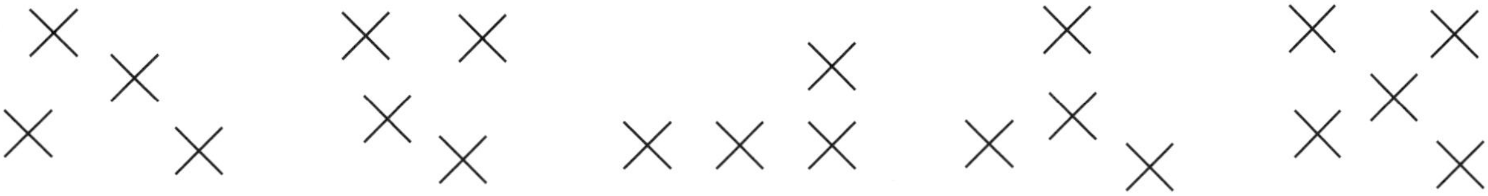

a b c d e

8

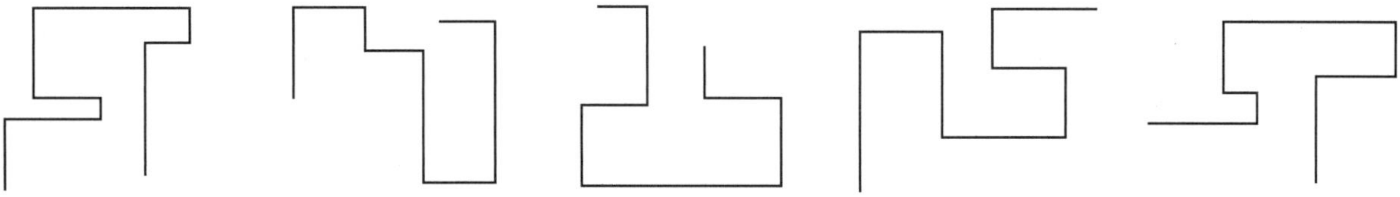

a b c d e

9

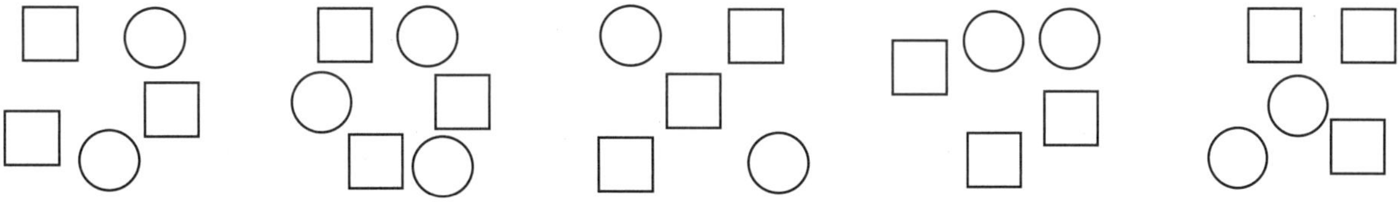

a b c d e

10

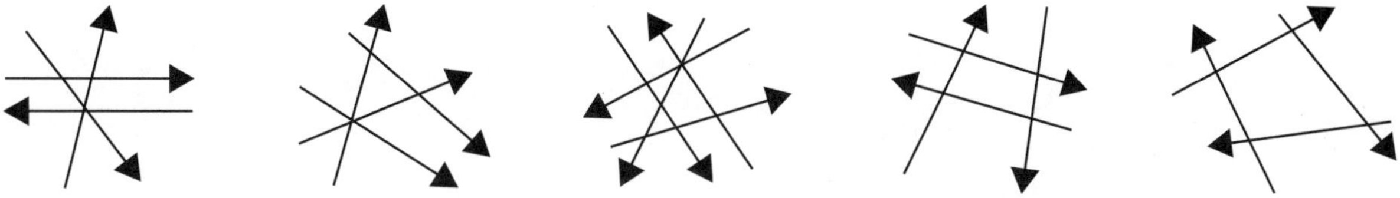

a b c d e

11

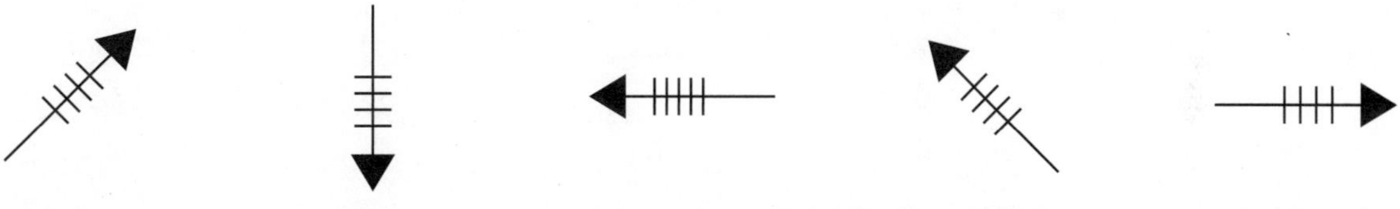

a b c d e

12

a b c d e

Which one comes next? Circle the letter.

Example

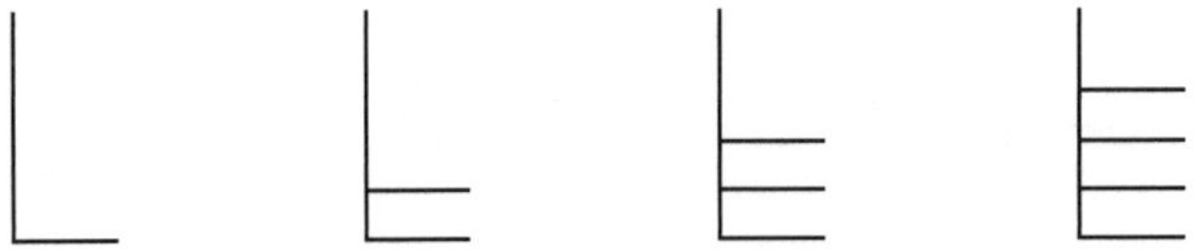

?

a b c (d) e

13

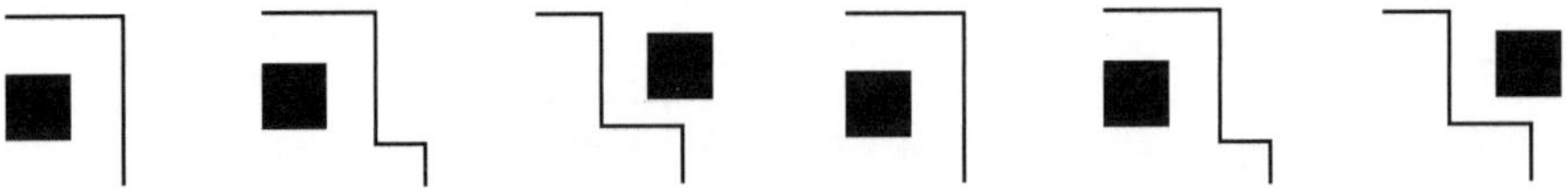

?

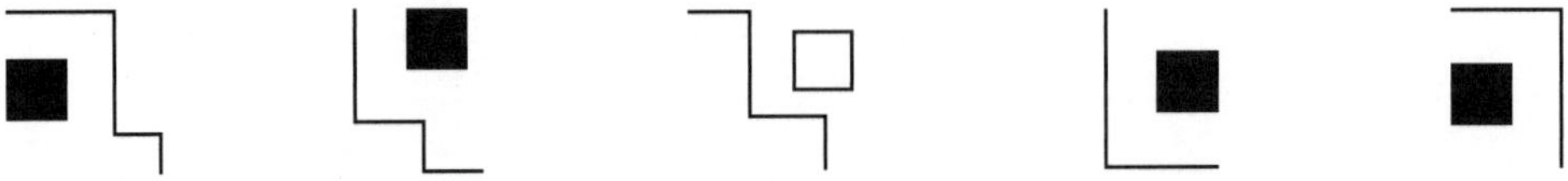

a b c d e

14

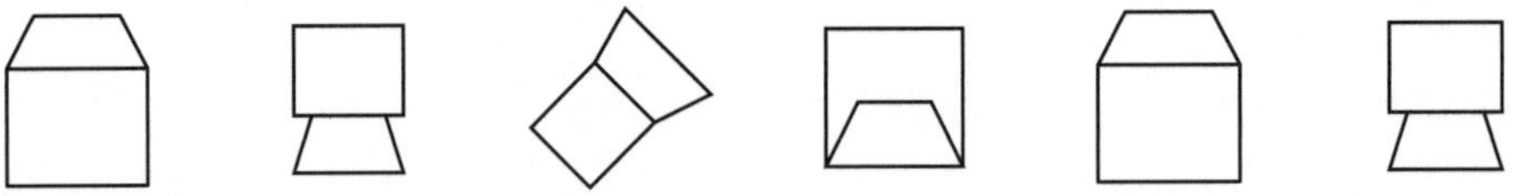

?

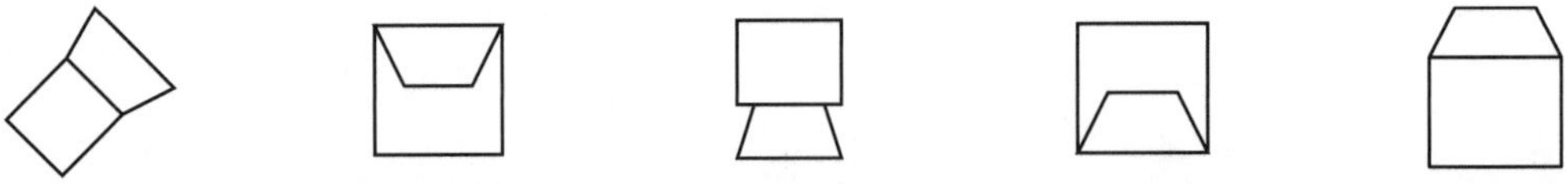

a b c d e

15

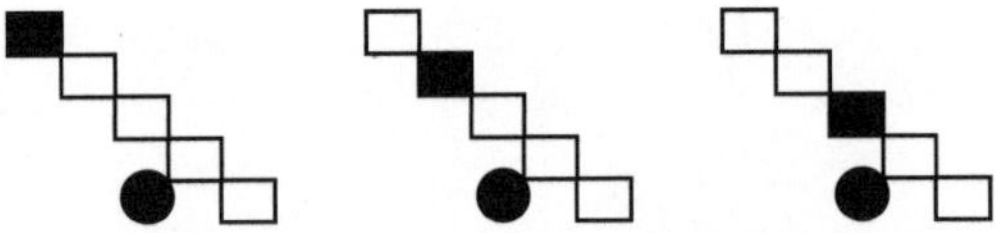

?

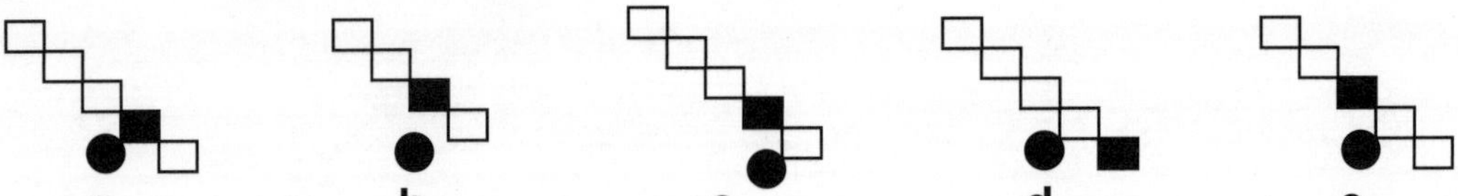

a b c d e

16

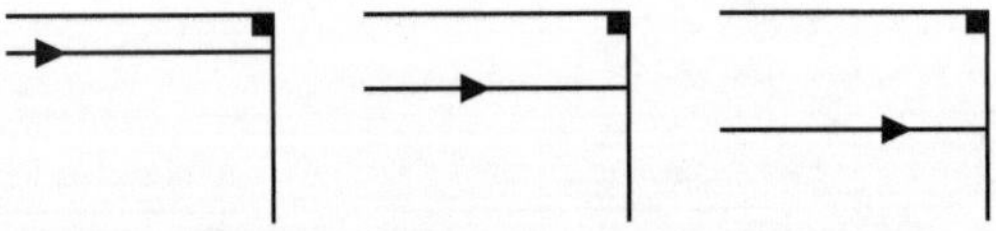

?

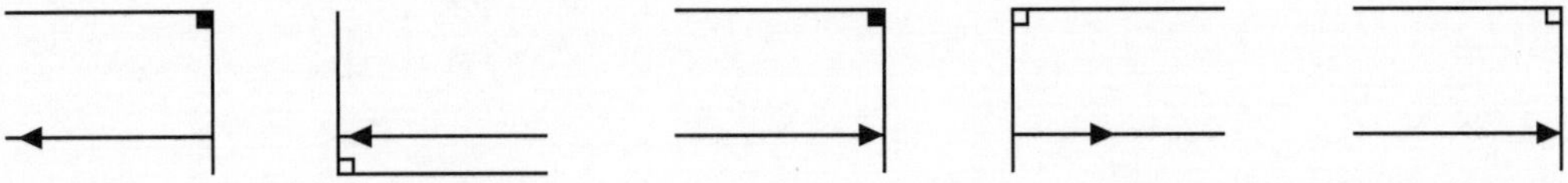

a b c d e

17

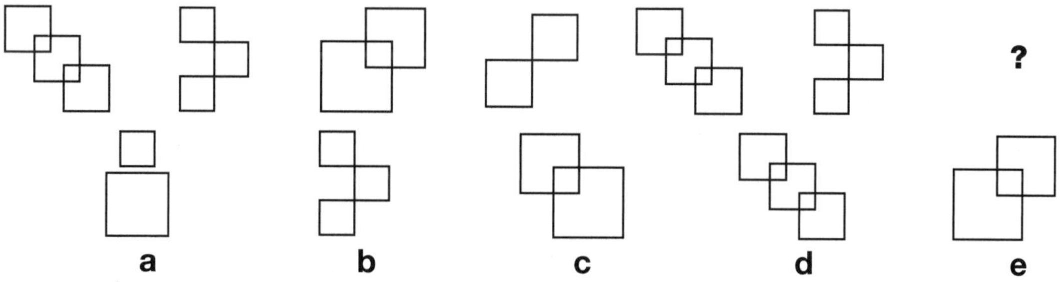

18

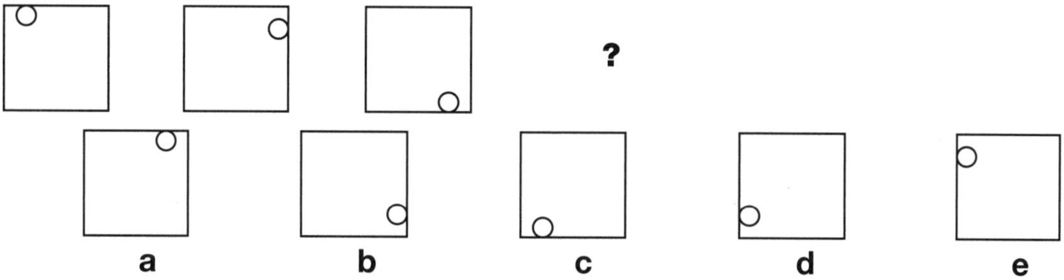

19

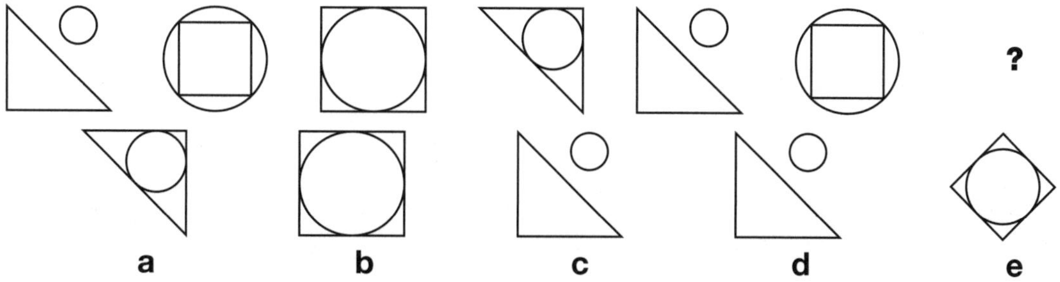

20

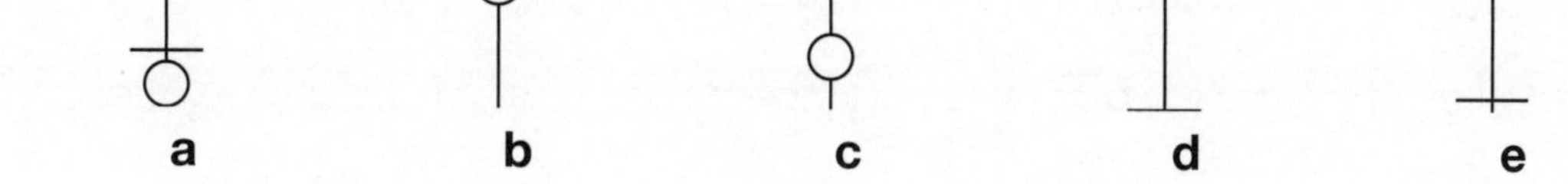

21
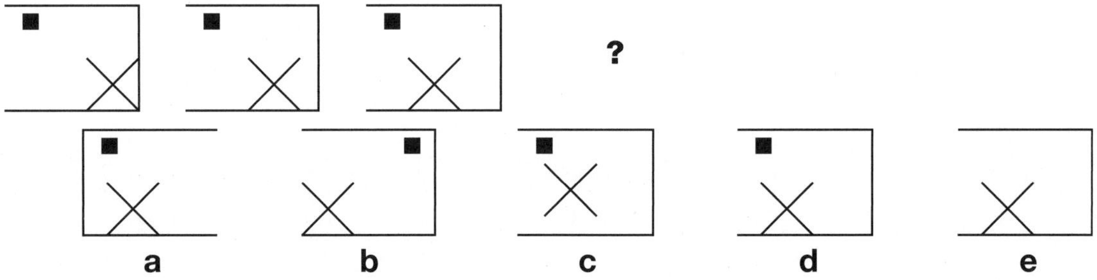

22
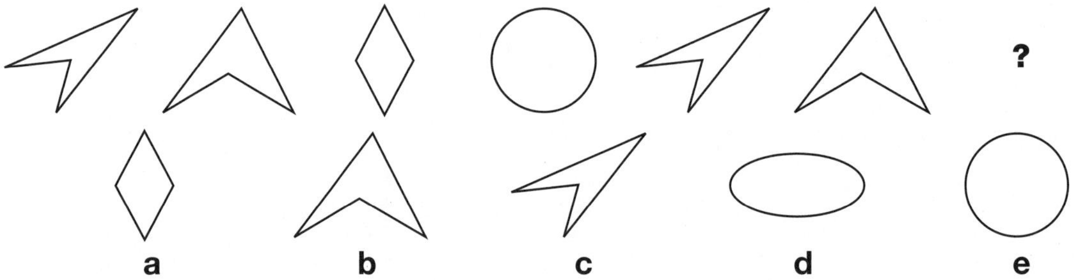

23
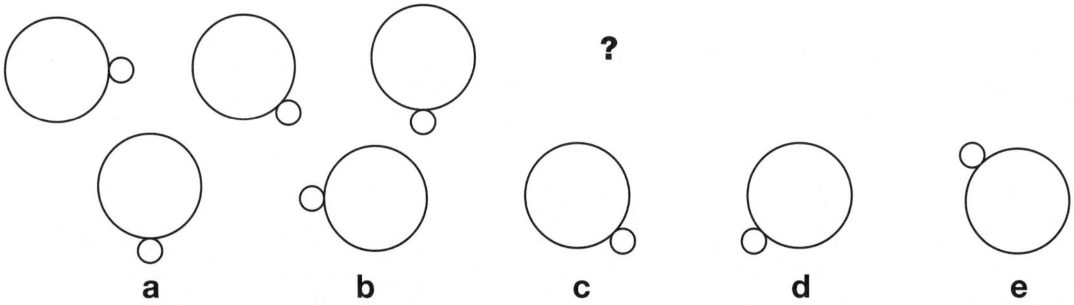

24
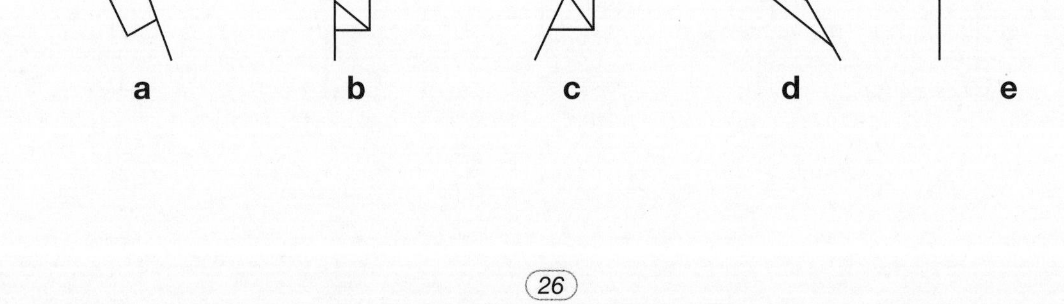

Which picture completes the second pair in the same way as the first pair?
Circle the letter.

Example

 is to  as  is to **?**

 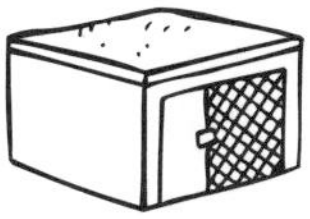   

a **b** **c** **d** **e**

25  is to 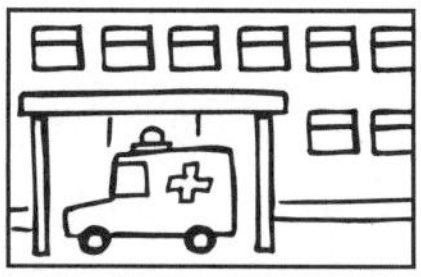 as  is to **?**

a **b** **c** **d** **e**

26 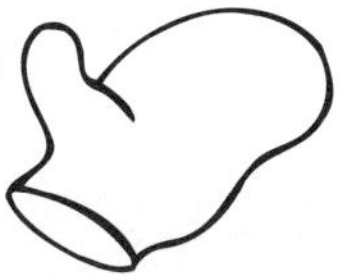 is to  as  is to **?**

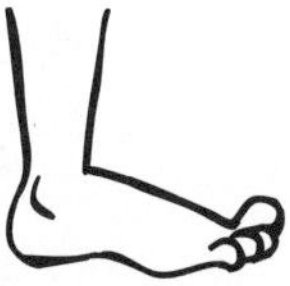    

a **b** **c** **d** **e**

27  is to 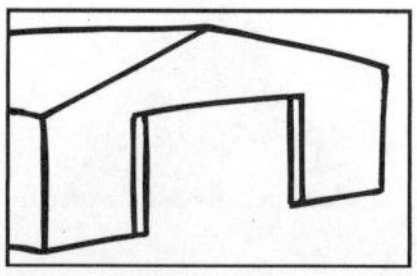 as  is to **?**

a **b** **c** **d** **e**

28

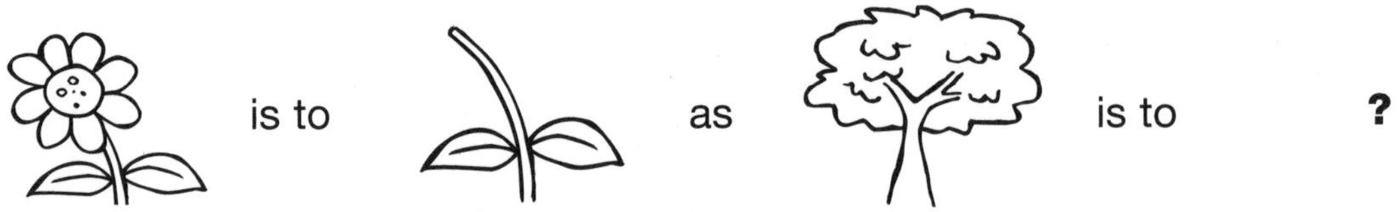

a **b** **c** **d** **e**

29

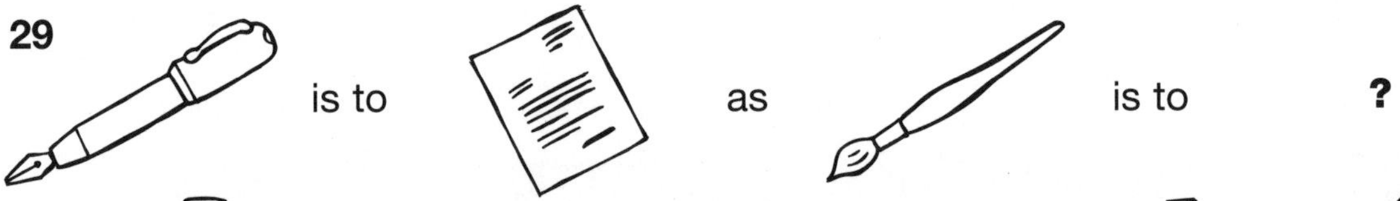

a **b** **c** **d** **e**

30

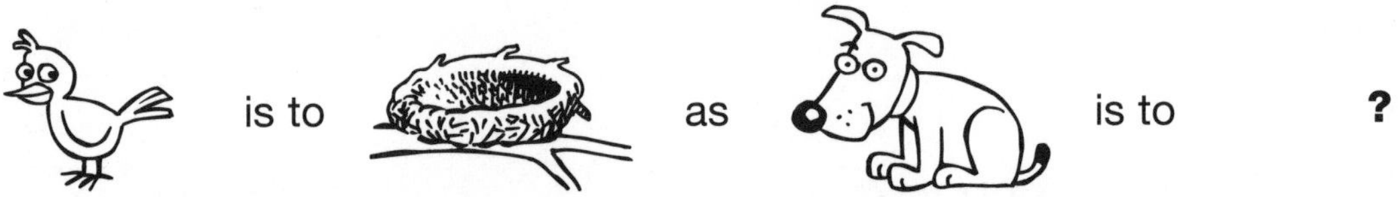

a **b** **c** **d** **e**

31

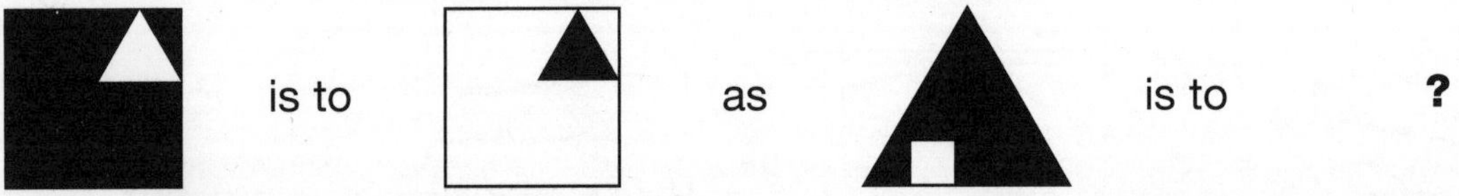

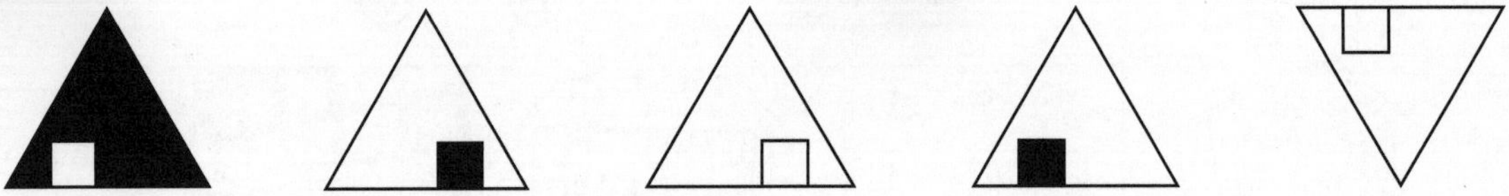

a **b** **c** **d** **e**

32
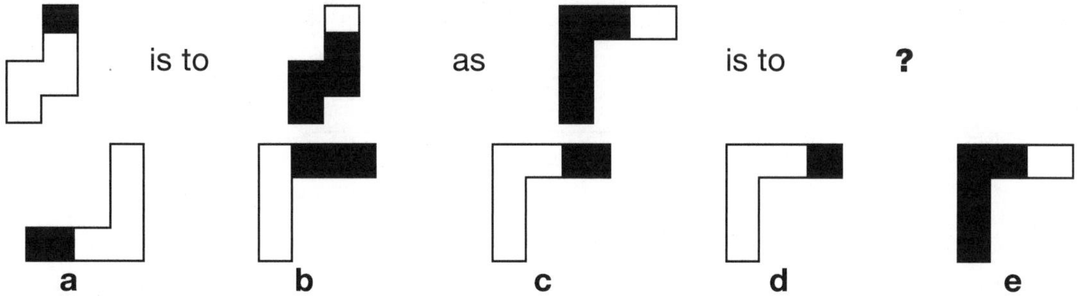
is to
as
is to
?
a
b
c
d
e

33
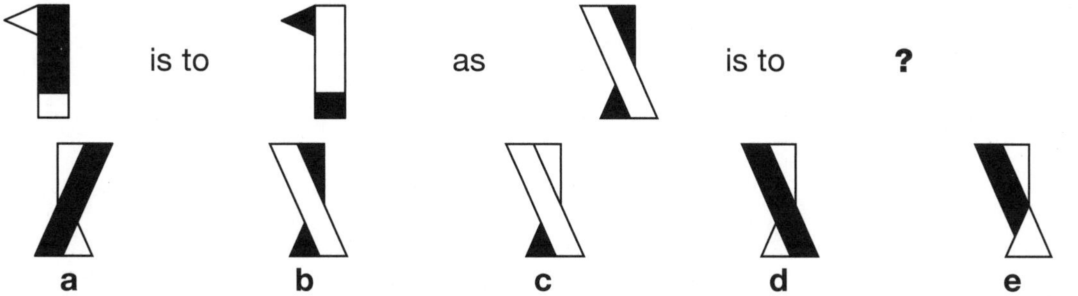
is to
as
is to
?
a
b
c
d
e

34
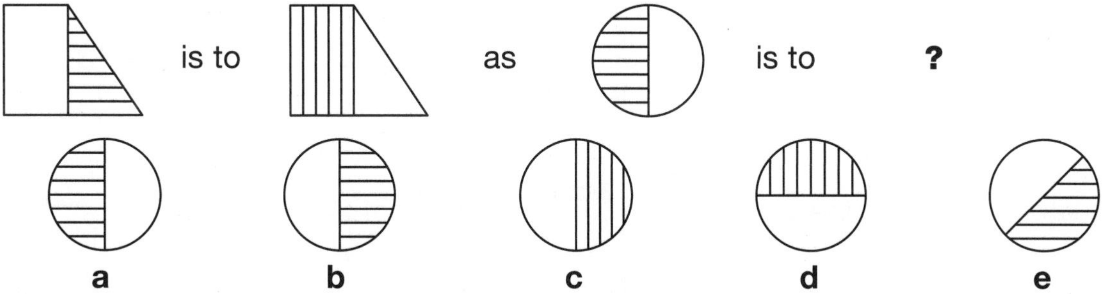
is to
as
is to
?
a
b
c
d
e

35
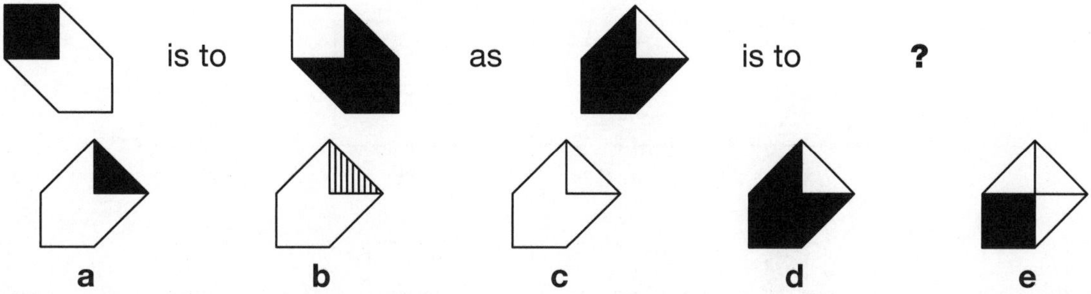
is to
as
is to
?
a
b
c
d
e

36
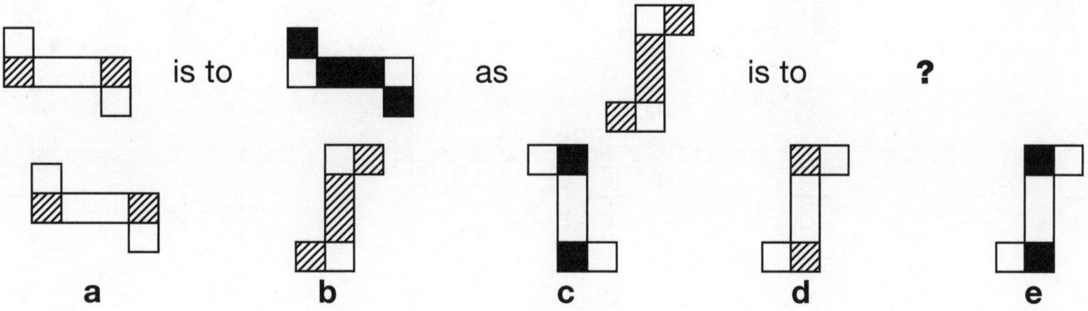
is to
as
is to
?
a
b
c
d
e

Which shape on the right is the reflection of the shape given on the left?
Circle the letter.

Example

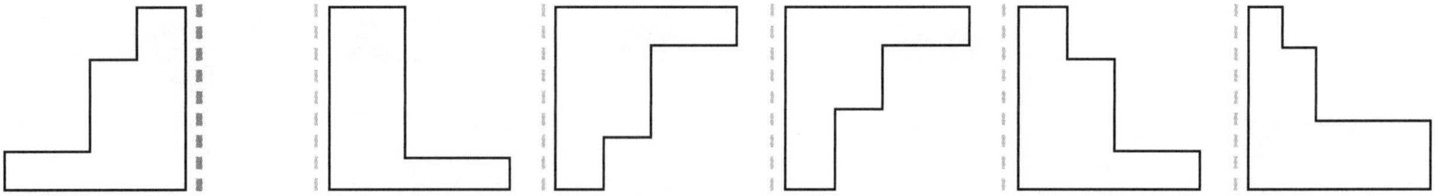

a b c d e

37

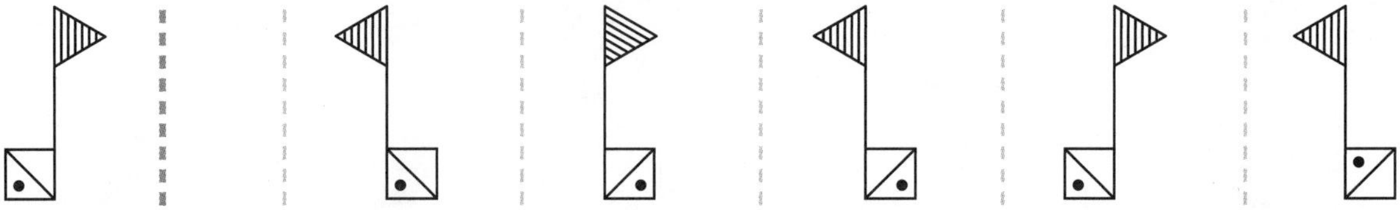

a b c d e

38

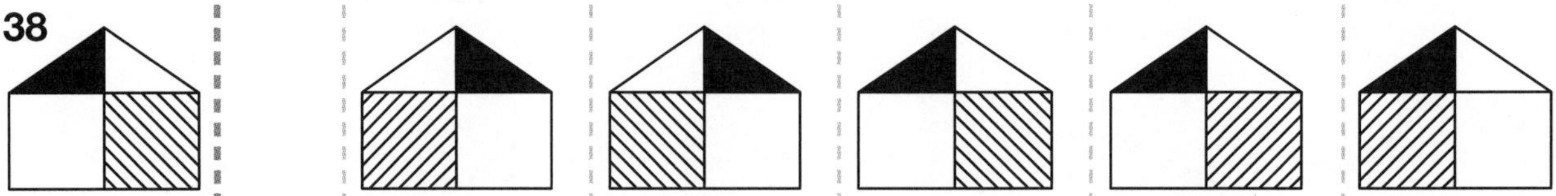

a b c d e

39

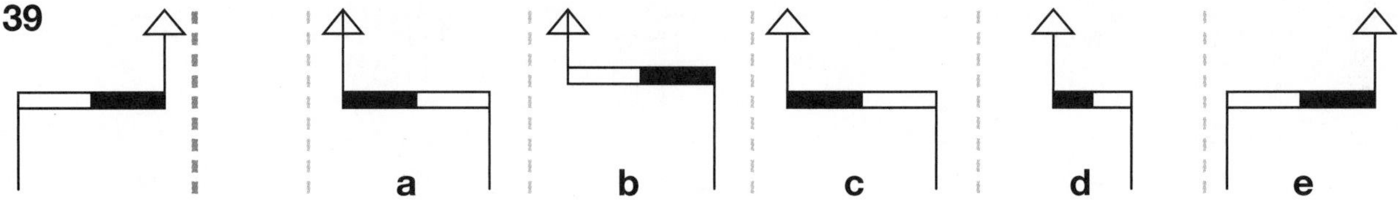

a b c d e

40

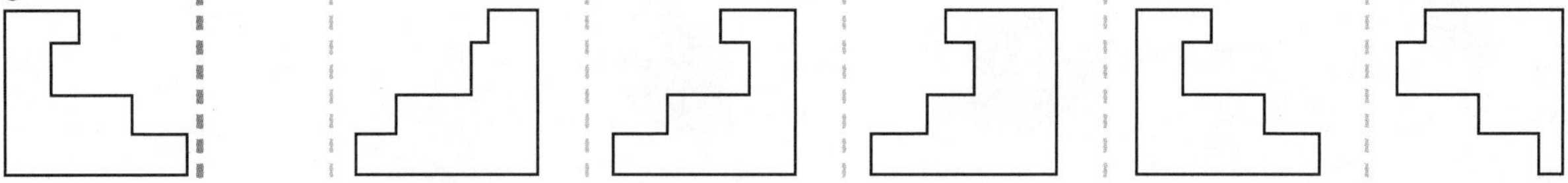

a b c d e

41

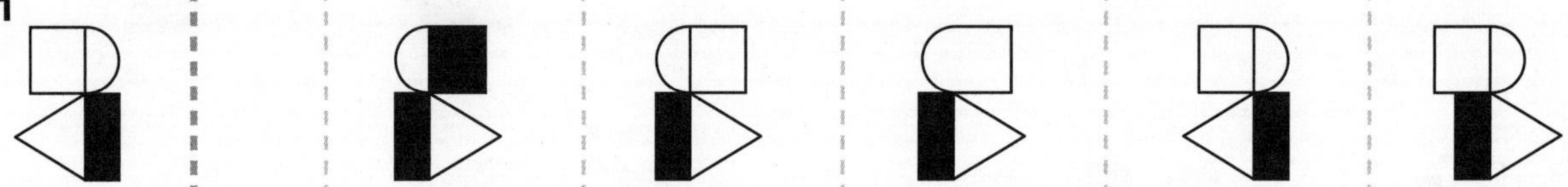

a b c d e

42

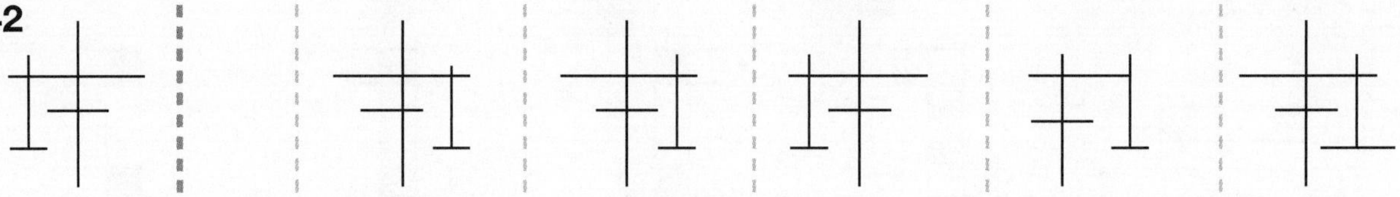

a b c d e

Paper 1 (pages 1–11)

1 **c** All of the pictures apart from c have a white door.
2 **a** All of the pictures apart from a have a white dollop of ice cream.
3 **c** All of the pictures apart from c have a white countertop.
4 **b** All of the pictures apart from b have four patterned patches.
5 **e** All of the pictures apart from e have a black eye patch.
6 **b** All of the pictures apart from b have grey petals.
7 **b** All of the shapes apart from b have a square inside a circle.
8 **c** All of the shapes apart from c have a circle touching the side of a triangle, not a vertex.
9 **d** All of the shapes apart from d have a short line close to the circle.
10 **a** All of the shapes apart from a have a black line close to the short side of the rectangle.
11 **a** All of the shapes apart from a have diagonal lines in the small centre square.
12 **b** All of the shapes apart from b have a circle inside a triangle.
13 **d** This is a chronological sequence of events showing a person visiting a post office.
14 **b** This is a chronological sequence of events showing a person hanging up laundry.
15 **d** This is a chronological sequence of events showing cookies being baked.
16 **a** This is a chronological sequence of events showing a people buying a kite and flying it.
17 **e** This is a chronological sequence of events showing a child receiving a gift and playing with it.
18 **b** The sequence is a repetition of the first four shapes: two squares alternate between being connected by a vertex and then overlapping, both horizontally and then vertically.
19 **e** The sequence is a repetition of the first four shapes: circle, triangle, square and pentagon.
20 **c** The sequence is a repetition of the first four shapes: cross, tick, pound sign and equals symbol.
21 **b** The sequence is a repetition of the first four shapes: right arrow, up arrow, diagonal arrow and down arrow.
22 **b** The sequence is a repetition of the first five shapes: four rectangles (with a diagonal line, then two perpendicular lines, then two diagonal lines, then no lines) and a circle with a diagonal line.
23 **a** The sequence is a repetition of the first four shapes: a small right-angled triangle, a triangle on its flat side, a triangle on its vertex and a larger right-angled triangle.
24 **b** The sequence is a repetition of the first four shapes: lined circle, dotty circle, circle with wiggly lines and a blank circle.
25 **d** The second picture is the trailer part of the first picture.
26 **e** The second picture is the ticket for the first picture.
27 **a** The second picture is the second part of the pair to the first picture.
28 **b** The second picture is a reflection of the first picture.
29 **d** The second picture is the crockery used for the food in the first picture.
30 **b** The second picture is the second part of the pair to the first picture.
31 **a** The second picture is the clothing worn on the body part in the first picture.
32 **a** The second picture is a reflection of the first picture.
33 **e** The second picture is a reflection of the first picture.
34 **e** The second picture is the habitat (including time of day) of the animal in the first picture.
35 **c** The second picture is a reflection of the first picture.
36 **b** The second picture is what the first picture grows into.

37 **a**

38 **b**

39 **c**

40 **c**

41 **a**

42 **c**

43 **a** The missing square will have a cow inside the square facing to the right.

44 **b** The missing square will have a card of the same suit as the top left square (spades), one lower in number (6).

45 **c** The missing square will be a vertical reflection of the bottom left square.

46 **a** The missing square will be a 180° rotation of the top left square.

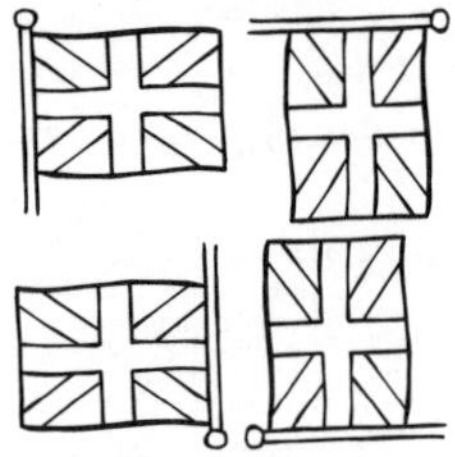

47 **e** The missing square will be same as the bottom left square.

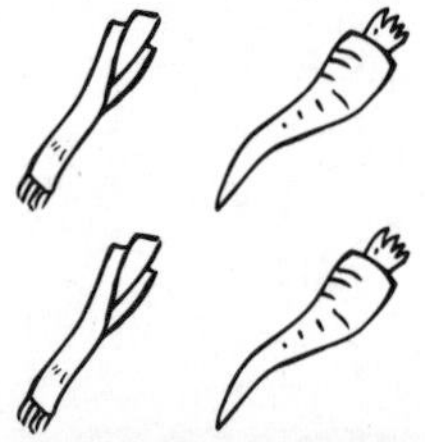

48 **e** The missing square will have one fewer animal than the top right square.

Paper 2 (pages 12–21)

1 **a** All of the pictures apart from a include a bike.
2 **e** All of the pictures apart from e have shoes.
3 **b** All of the pictures apart from b have six cards.
4 **c** All of the pictures apart from c nine flowers.
5 **d** All of the pictures apart from d have four bars in the chair.
6 **b** All of the pictures apart from b have five wheels in total.
7 **c** All of the patterns apart from c have one bigger circle and one smaller square.
8 **a** All of the patterns apart from a have another shape inside the triangle.
9 **c** All of the patterns apart from c have one bigger striped square and one smaller white triangle.
10 **c** All of the patterns apart from c have a shorter rectangle.
11 **a** All of the patterns apart from a have a shorter line.
12 **d** All of the patterns apart from d have the middle straight line facing into the 'U' shape.
13 **c** This is a chronological sequence of events showing children playing on a slide.
14 **e** This is a chronological sequence of events showing biscuits being made.
15 **a** This is a chronological sequence of events showing a person mowing the lawn.
16 **e** This is a chronological sequence of events showing a house being built.
17 **e** The number of backward C shapes in the bottom of row decreases by one each time.
18 **d** One line is added each time.
19 **e** The number of circles decreased by one each time; the number of crosses stays the same.
20 **e** The number of V shapes on the end of the arrow increases by one each time.
21 **b** The number of both black and white circles decreases by one each time.
22 **e** The number of horizontal lines decreases by one each time.
23 **b** The number of arrows increases by one each time; the circle stays in the same place.
24 **d** The number of crosses increases by one each time; the number of black squares stays the same.
25 **d** The second shape has the same number of sides as the first shape but they are all the same length.
26 **b** The small shape inside the second square is in the opposite corner compared to its position in the first square.
27 **b** The second shape is a 90° clockwise rotation of the first shape.
28 **a** The second shape is a 90° anti-clockwise rotation of the first shape.
29 **d** The pattern in the second shape is at the opposite end of the rectangle compared to its position in the first shape.
30 **d** The second shape has the same number of sides as the first shape and is the 'complete' version of the first shape.

31 **a** The second shape is the same as the first shape but has swapped the triangles for semi-circles.
32 **b** The small shape inside the second triangle has been moved to the bottom right corner.
33 **b** The second shape is a 180° rotation of the first shape.
34 **d** The flag in the second shape has moved down slightly compared to its position in the first shape.
35 **c** The second pattern has the same two shapes as the first pattern, but the inner shape has become the outer shape and vice versa.
36 **c** The second shape is a 90° clockwise rotation of the first shape.
37 **e**

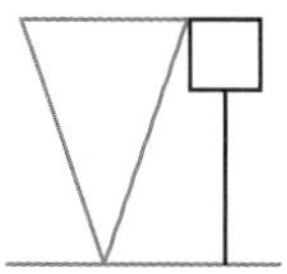

38 **c**

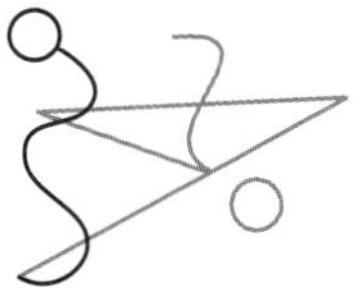

39 **a**

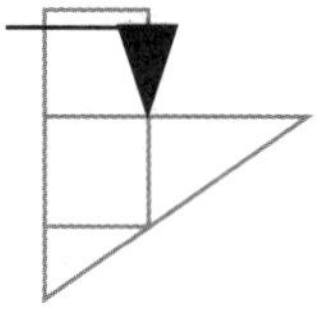

40 **d**

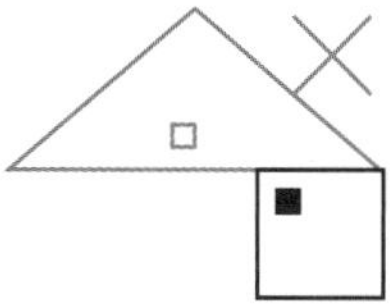

41 **b**

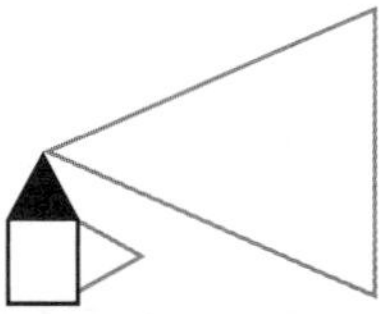

42 **b**

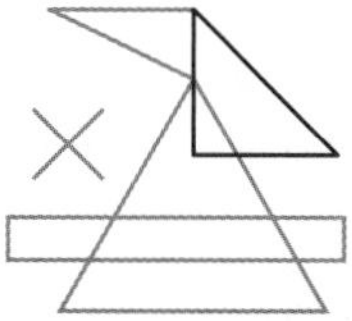

43–48 When each shape is paired with the correct reflection, they form a single shape that is perfectly symmetrical.
43 **a**

44 **e**

45 **a**

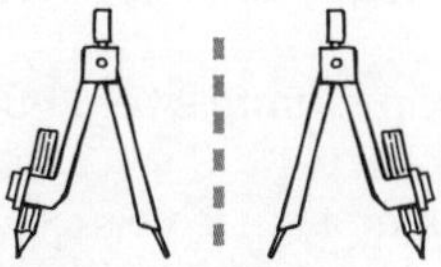

46 **b**

47 **d**

48 **c**

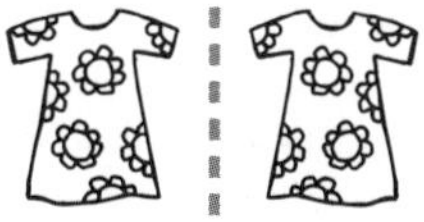

Paper 3 (pages 22–32)

1 **e** All of the pictures apart from e are of phones.
2 **a** All of the pictures apart from a are of tools.
3 **b** All of the pictures apart from b are painting implements.
4 **d** All of the pictures apart from d are items used to help you see.
5 **e** All of the pictures apart from e are of items which hold drink.
6 **d** All of the pictures apart from d are of gardening tools.
7 **e** All of the patterns apart from e are made up of four crosses.
8 **a** All of the shapes apart from a are made up of eight straight lines.
9 **b** All of the patterns apart from b are made up of two circles and three squares.
10 **c** All of the patterns apart from c are made up of four arrows.
11 **c** All of the shapes apart from c have four short lines on each arrow.
12 **c** All of the patterns apart from c have three long horizontal lines and one short vertical line.
13 **e** The sequence is a repetition of the first three shapes.
14 **a** The sequence is a repetition of the first four shapes.
15 **a** The black rectangle moves down one place in each new shape; the black circle stays in the same place.
16 **c** The lower horizontal line moves down each time; the arrowhead moves to the right each time.
17 **e** The sequence is a repetition of the first four shapes.
18 **d** The shape rotates 90° clockwise each time.
19 **b** The sequence is a repetition of the first four shapes.
20 **e** The horizontal line moves down each time; the circle stays the same.
21 **d** The cross moves to the left each time; the small black rectangle stays the same.
22 **a** The sequence is a repetition of the first four shapes.
23 **d** The small circle moves clockwise around the large circle, 45° each time.

24 **e** The sequence is a repetition of the first three shapes.
25 **b** The second picture is the building where the person in the first picture works.
26 **a** The second picture is the body part that wears the clothing in the first picture.
27 **e** The second picture is the place in which the method of transport in the first picture is stored.
28 **d** The second picture is the lower half of the first picture.
29 **c** The second picture is what is created using the item in the first picture.
30 **b** The second picture is where the animal in the first picture sleeps.
31 **d** The second shape is the same as the first shape but with the colours swapped.
32 **c** The second shape is the same as the first shape but with the colours swapped.
33 **d** The second shape is the same as the first shape but with the colours swapped.
34 **c** The second shape is the same as the first shape but with the lines moved to the other half of the shape and rotated to vertical.
35 **a** The second shape is the same as the first shape but with the colours swapped.
36 **e** The second shape is the same as the first shape but the white parts have become black and the hatched parts have become white.
37–42 When each shape is paired with the correct reflection, they form a single shape that is perfectly symmetrical.
37 **c**

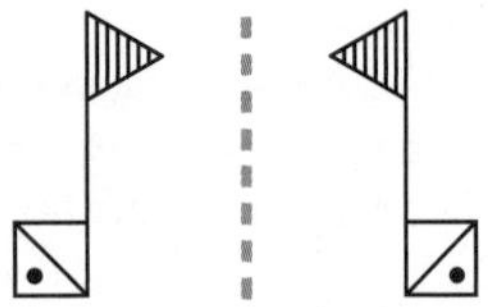

38 **a**

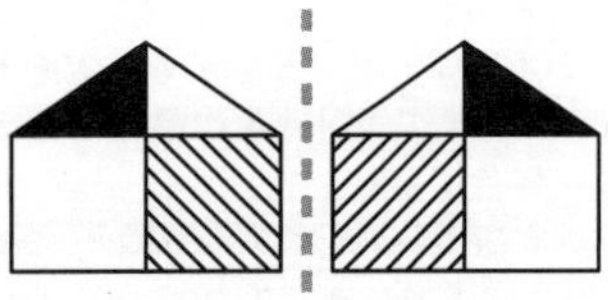

39 **c**

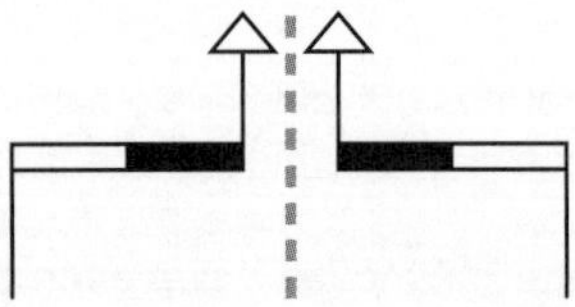

40 **b**

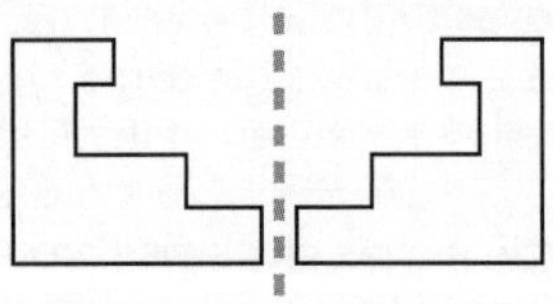

41 **b**

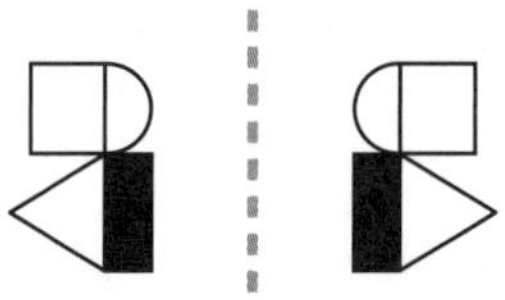

42 **b**

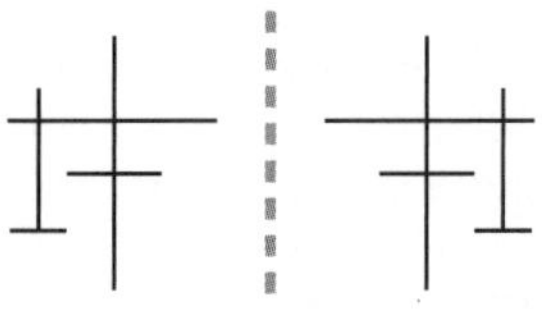

43 **d** The first letter represents the petals (R has five petals, S has six petals and T has four petals). The second letter represents the centre pattern (J has a white centre, K has a black centre and L has a dotted centre).
44 **e** The first letter represents the windows (A has one window, B has two windows and C has three windows). The second letter represents the roof (P has no roof, Q has a three-sided roof and R has a two-sided roof).
45 **c** The first letter represents the top of the tie (L has a rectangle, M has a circle and N has a trapezium). The second letter represents the pattern (P has stripes, Q has dots and R is blank).
46 **e** The first letter represents the size of the circle (F has a small circle, G has a medium circle and H has a large circle). The second letter represents the pattern (X has grey shading, Y has vertical lines and Z has crosses).
47 **b** The first letter represents the line of the arrow (T has a large rectangle, U has a small rectangle and V is just a line). The second letter represents the triangle (J has a grey triangle, K has a white triangle and L has a white triangle with a horizontal line).
48 **d** The first letter represents the shape (B has a triangle, C has a circle and D has a square). The second letter represents the size of the shape (F has a large shape, G has a medium shape and H has a small shape).

Paper 4 (pages 33–42)

1 **a** All of the pictures apart from a are play park equipment.
2 **e** All of the pictures apart from e are kitchen implements.
3 **e** All of the pictures apart from e are rubbish bins.
4 **c** All of the pictures apart from c are indoor chairs.
5 **c** All of the shapes apart from c are squares.
6 **a** All of the shapes apart from a have a white section.

7 **b** All of the patterns apart from b have a white shape.
8 **b** All of the shapes apart from b are circles.
9 **d** All of the shapes apart from d are triangles.
10 **e** All of the patterns apart from e have a white square in the middle.
11 **a** All of the shapes apart from a are white.
12 **e** All of the shapes apart from e are quadrilaterals.
13 **c** This is a chronological sequence of events showing a person having a haircut.
14 **b** This is a chronological sequence of events showing the life cycle of a frog.
15 **d** This is a chronological sequence of events showing a person cooking burgers.
16 **c** This is a chronological sequence of events showing how to make papier maché.
17 **b** This is a chronological sequence of events showing a person getting ready in the morning.
18 **d** The black circle rotates anti-clockwise around each point of the star.
19 **a** The two vertical lines move further up the diagonal line each time.
20 **d** The square that starts at top middle moves one square clockwise each time; the dot in the bottom left square stays the same.
21 **b** The cross moves clockwise around each corner of the shape.
22 **d** The small black triangle moves clockwise round each side of the bigger triangle.
23 **a** The arrowhead moves down and to the right each time.
24 **e** The small black square moves clockwise around the larger square each time, from corner, to side, to corner.
25 **b** The second shape is the bottom half of the first shape.
26 **c** The second shape is the same as the first shape but the colours have been swapped.
27 **e** The second shape is a smaller version of the first shape.
28 **b** The second shape is a 180° rotation of the first shape, and has become black.
29 **b** The second shape is the same as the first shape but the black has become dark grey and the light grey has become medium grey; the white has remained the same.
30 **c** The second shape is the shape with vertices shown by the crosses in the first shape.
31 **e** The second pattern has the same two types of small inner shapes as the first pattern; it has one more of one type of shape and one fewer of the other type of shape than the first pattern.
32 **a** The second pattern is the same as the first pattern but the small white shape has become black and the small medium grey shape has become light grey.
33 **b** In the second pattern, the central line has become shorter and the small shape on the left of the line has increased in size; the small shape on the right of the line stays the same.
34 **e** The second shape is the same as the first shape but the white has become black and the black has become grey.
35 **a** The second shape has three times as many of the small shapes at each end of the line.
36 **a** In the second pattern, the outer shape has decreased in size and the inner shape has increased in size.
37 **a** The missing square is a vertical reflection of the bottom left square.

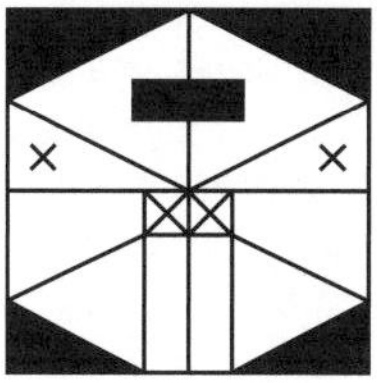

38 **a** The missing square is a horizontal reflection of the top right square.

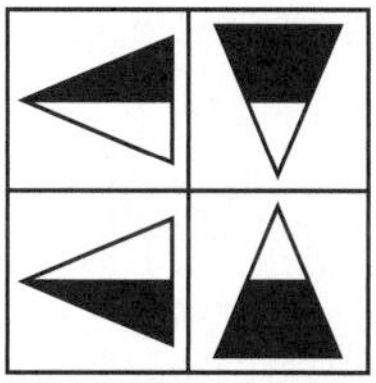

39 **c** The missing square is a reflection of the diagonally opposite square.

40 **d** The missing square is a horizontal reflection of the top right square.

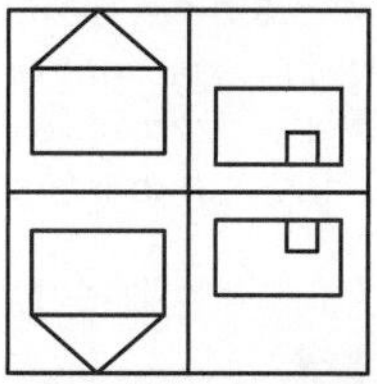

41 **e** The missing square is a reflection of the diagonally opposite square.

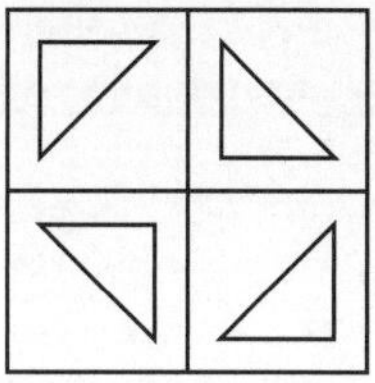

42 **c** The missing square is a 90° clockwise rotation of the top right square.

43 **c** The first letter represents the larger shape (A has a triangle, B has a quadrilateral with two right angles and C has a quadrilateral with one right angle). The second letter represents the position of the circle (J has the circle in the bottom left corner, K has it more in the centre and L has it overlapping the edge of the larger shape).

44 **b** The first letter represents the direction of the line (D has a vertical line, E has a horizontal line and F has a diagonal line). The second letter represents the number of arrowheads on the line (N has two arrowheads, O has one and M has three).

45 **e** The first letter represents the size of the rectangle (F has as large rectangle, G has a medium rectangle and H has a small rectangle). The second letter represents the colour (R has medium grey shading, S has white shading and T has light grey shading).

46 **d** The first letter represents the direction of the line (X has a has a diagonal line, Y has a horizontal line and Z has a vertical line). The second letter represents the position of the small dashes (P has the dashes at the centre of the line, Q has the dashes near the end of the line and R has the dashes at the end of the line).

47 **d** The first letter represents the number of squares (U has three squares, V has one and W has two). The second letter represents the shading (L has diagonal lines, M has white shading and N has black shading).

48 **c** The first letter represents the shape (G has a square, H has a circle and I has a triangle). The second letter represents the size of the shape (A has a small shape, B has a medium shape and C has a large shape).

Paper 5 (pages 43–52)

1 **e** All of the pictures apart from e are adults.
2 **b** All of the pictures apart from b are small birds.
3 **c** All of the pictures apart from c have a human smaller than the vehicle.
4 **b** All of the pictures apart from b are large animals.
5 **c** All of the shapes apart from c have only one pair of perpendicular lines.
6 **e** All of the shapes apart from e are made from only two triangles.
7 **a** All of the circles apart from a have only three crosses on the circumference.
8 **b** All of the shapes apart from b are made from perpendicular lines.
9 **e** All of the shapes apart from e have one vertical and one horizontal arrow.
10 **d** All of the shapes apart from d have two small circles and three crosses on the edge.
11 **c** All of the shapes apart from c have four loops.
12 **c** All of the shapes apart from c contain only right angles.
13 **e** The sequence is a repetition of the first four shapes.
14 **c** The sequence is a repetition of the first four shapes.
15 **d** The circle gets larger each time.
16 **d** The square gets larger each time.
17 **b** The sequence is a repetition of the first four shapes.
18 **c** The circle gets smaller each time; the square stays the same size.
19 **d** The sequence is a repetition of the first four shapes.
20 **b** The triangle on the left gets smaller each time; the other triangle stays the same size.
21 **c** The number of black squares decreases by one each time; the number of white squares stays the same.
22 **e** The sequence is a repetition of the first four shapes.
23 **a** The number of horizontal lines decreases by one each time.
24 **c** The sequence is a repetition of the first three shapes.
25 **d** The second picture is the prey of the animal in the first picture.
26 **d** The second picture is where the food in the first picture is stored.
27 **a** The second picture is a close up of the weather in the first picture.
28 **b** The second picture is the terrain on which the machine in the first picture is used.
29 **b** The second picture is the means of transport for the person in the first picture.
30 **e** The second picture is what can be made from the material in the first picture.
31 **d** The second shape is the same as the first.
32 **e** In the second shape, the small shape inside the larger shape has moved lower down.
33 **c** In the second shape, the short vertical line has moved to the base.
34 **e** In the second shape, the small item under the 'table' has moved to the top.
35 **d** In the second shape, the inner pattern of lines at the base of the arrow has moved further towards the arrowhead.

36 **b** In the second shape, the arrows are aligned to the right.

37 **a**

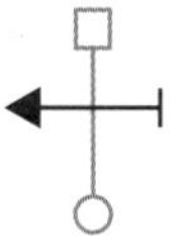

38 **d**

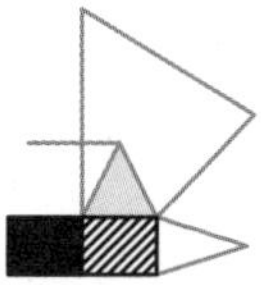

39 **b**

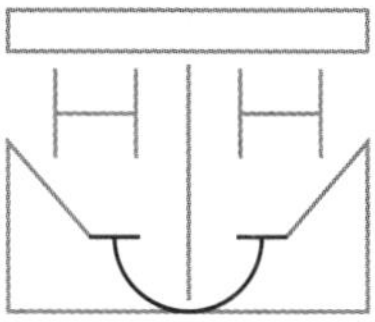

40 **c**

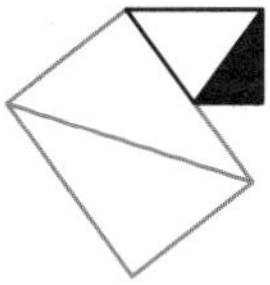

41 **d**

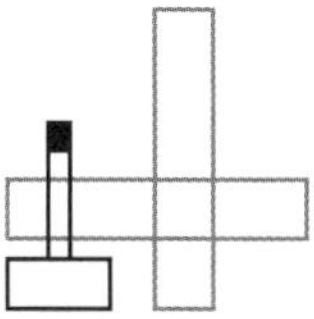

42 **b**

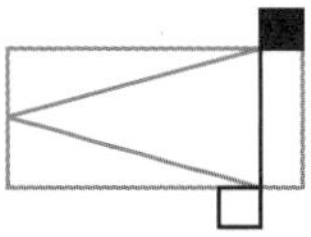

43–48 When each shape is paired with the correct reflection, they form a single shape that is perfectly symmetrical.

43 **e**

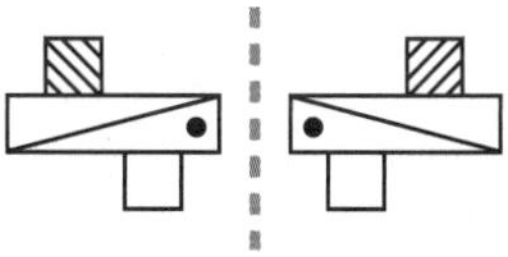

44 **b**

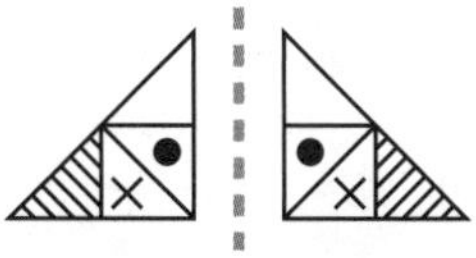

45 **c**

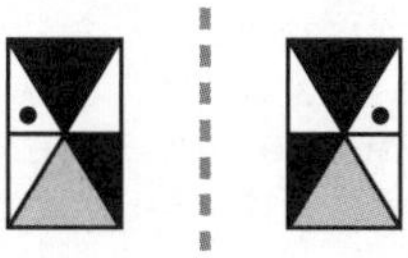

46 **c**

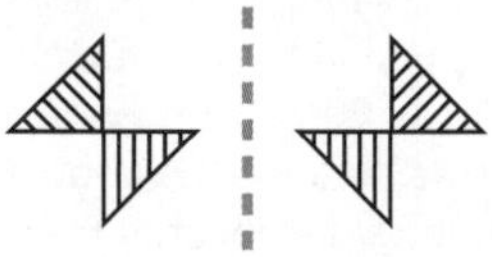

47 **a**

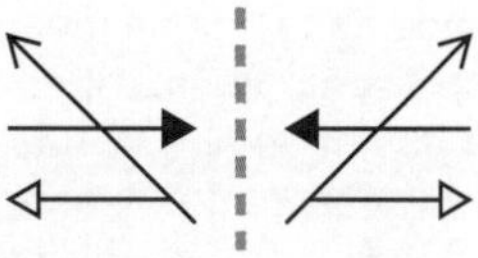

48 **e**

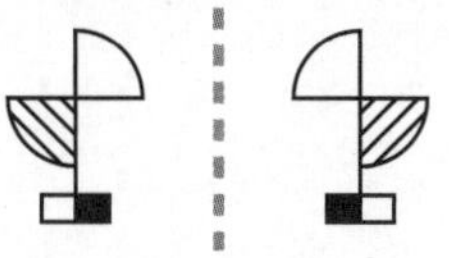

Paper 6 (pages 53–63)

1 **a** All of the pictures apart from a has the second item from the left shaded in grey.
2 **d** All of the pictures apart from d has an L plate to the left of the registration plate.
3 **b** All of the pictures apart from b have a hand sticking out to the left of the person's face.
4 **d** All of the pictures apart from d have a hat on the person's head.
5 **b** All of the shapes apart from b are triangles.
6 **e** All of the shapes apart from e have a small square on the vertex of a hexagon.
7 **e** All of the shapes apart from e have two different 'windows' – one square and one rectangular.
8 **d** All of the shapes apart from d have one square and one triangle.
9 **c** All of the shapes apart from c have two rectangles of different sizes.
10 **d** All of the patterns apart from d have the white and black circles in the same position.
11 **e** All of the patterns apart from e have an arrow to the left of the wiggly line.
12 **a** All of the shapes apart from a have one square and one semicircle.
13 **d** This is a chronological sequence of events showing a pizza being made.
14 **a** This is a chronological sequence of events showing a snowy scene.
15 **d** This is a chronological sequence of events showing a group of people going to the beach.
16 **e** This is a chronological sequence of events showing people competing in a sack race.
17 **b** This is a chronological sequence of events showing a picture being painted.
18 **c** This is a chronological sequence of events showing a spider spinning its web.
19 **c** The sequence is a repetition of the first three shapes.
20 **b** The sequence is a repetition of the first four shapes.
21 **d** The sequence is a repetition of the first three shapes: a quadrilateral, a triangle and a circle.
22 **c** The sequence is a repetition of the first four shapes.
23 **a** The sequence is a repetition of the first four shapes.
24 **e** The sequence is a repetition of the first three shapes.
25 **d** The second picture is a vertical reflection of the first shape.
26 **b** The second picture is a vertical reflection of the first shape.
27 **e** The second picture is a vertical reflection of the first shape.

28 **d** The second picture is a vertical reflection of the first shape.
29 **c** In the second shape, the circles at the vertices have become triangles.
30 **d** The second shape is a 180° rotation of the first shape.
31 **a** The second shape is 90° clockwise rotation of the first shape.
32 **c** The second shape is the same as the first shape but with the outermost sides missing.
33 **a** The second shape is the first shape combined with its horizontal reflection, with the vertical line omitted in the reflection.
34 **e** The second shape is a 180° rotation of the first shape.
35 **c** The second shape is 90° clockwise rotation of the first shape.
36 **b** The second shape is a 'block' version of the first shape.
37 **b** The missing square will be a vertical reflection of the top left square.

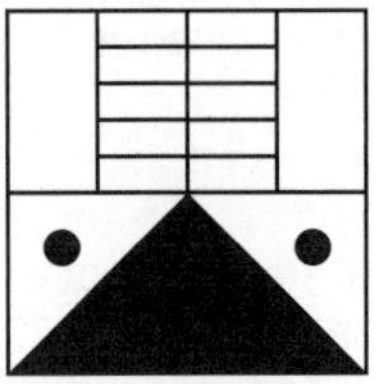

38 **d** The missing square will be a 90° clockwise rotation of the top right square.

39 **e** The missing square will be the same as the bottom left square.

40 **b** The missing square will contain three small black triangles.

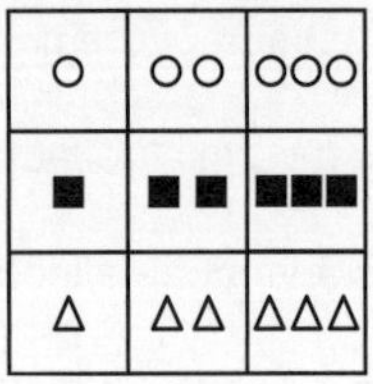

41 **d** The missing square will be the same as the top right square.

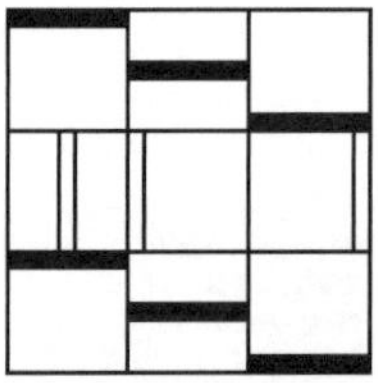

42 **a** The missing square will be the same as the middle square, with a horizontal line added.

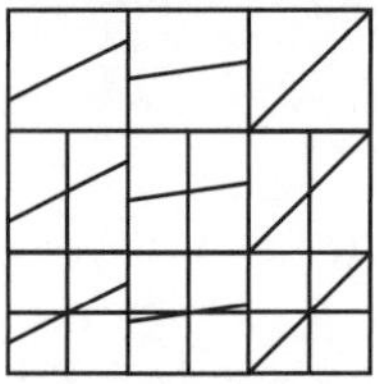

43 **b** The first letter represents the shape (A has circles, B has triangles and C has squares). The second letter represents the number of shapes (J has two shapes, K has one and L has three).
44 **d** The first letter represents the position of the shape across three distinct levels (F has the shape at the top level, G has the shape at the bottom level and H has the shape in the middle). The second letter represents the shading of the shape (R has white shading, S has black shading and T has diagonal stripes).
45 **e** The first letter represents the direction of the straight line (X has a horizontal line, Y has a diagonal line and Z has a vertical line). The second letter represents the circle at the end of the line (P has a small black circle, Q has a medium white circle and R has a large white circle).
46 **d** The first letter represents the shading of the shape (G has black shading, H has white shading and I has diagonal stripes). The second letter represents the letter the shape makes (A has a T shape, B has an L shape and C has a V shape).
47 **a** The first letter represents the position of the shape across three distinct levels (D has the shape at the top level, E has the shape in the middle and F has the shape at the bottom level). The second letter represents the length of the shape (M has a short shape, N has a medium-length shape and O has a long shape).
48 **e** The first letter represents the number of dots (U has two dots, V has three and W has four). The second letter represents the direction of the line of dots (L has a horizontal line of dots, M has a vertical line of dots and N has a diagonal line of dots).

Which code matches the shape or pattern given at the end of each line. Circle the letter.

Example

AX AY BZ CY BX ?

a BZ **b** AZ **c** CX **d** BY **e** CZ

43

RJ TL SK SJ TK ?

a SL **b** RK **c** TJ **d** RL **e** TL

44

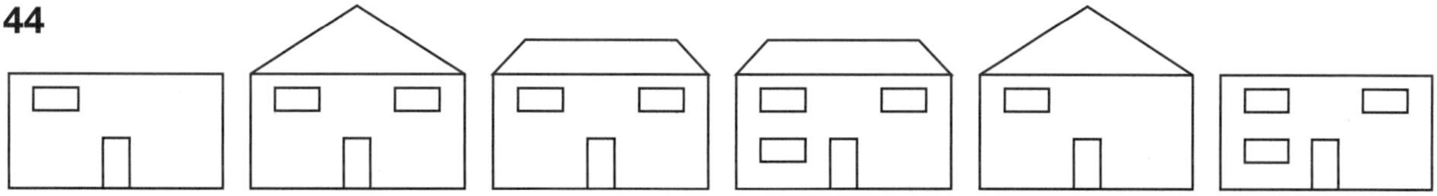

AP BR BQ CQ AR ?

a CR **b** BP **c** AQ **d** CQ **e** CP

45

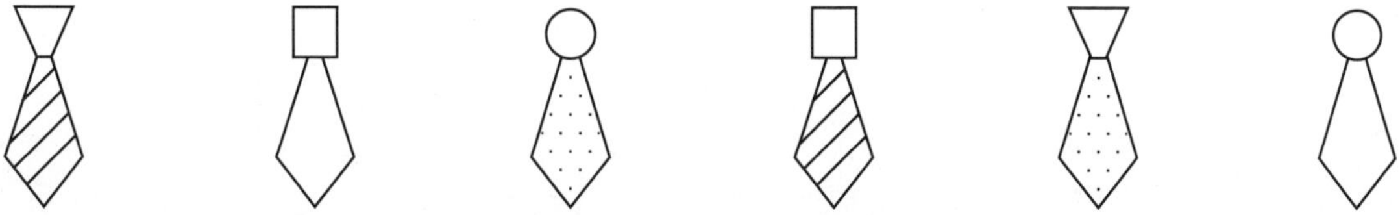

NP LR MQ LP NQ ?

a MP **b** LQ **c** MR **d** MQ **e** NR

46

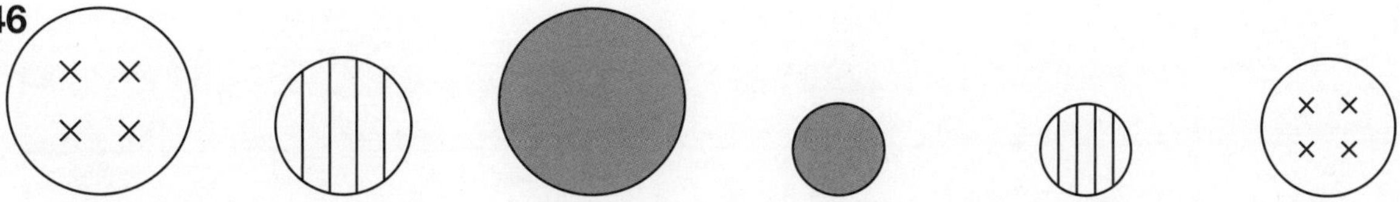

HZ GY HX FX FY ?

a HZ **b** GX **c** FZ **d** HY **e** GZ

47

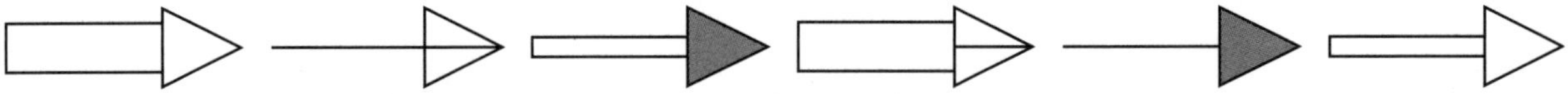

TK VL UJ TL VJ **?**

a UL **b** UK **c** VK **d** TK **e** TJ

48

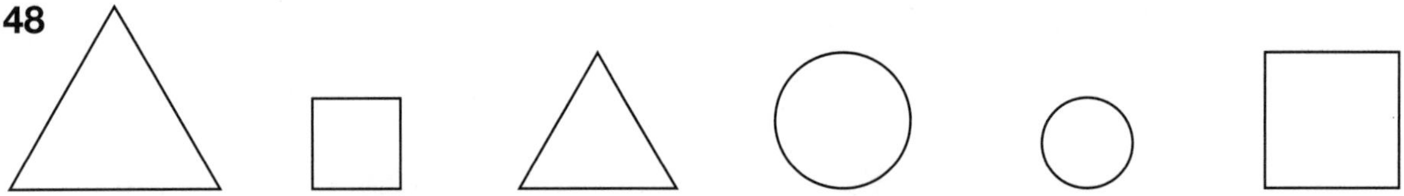

BF DH BG CG CH **?**

a DF **b** CF **c** DH **d** DG **e** BH

Now go to the Progress Chart to record your score! **Total** ◯ **48**

Paper 4

Which is the odd one out? Circle the letter.

Example

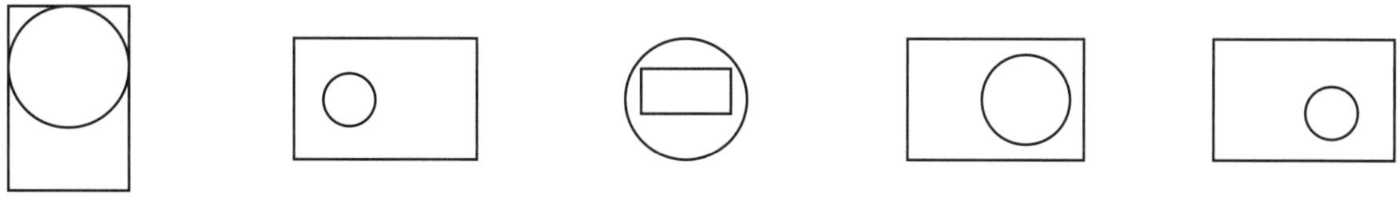

a b (c) d e

1

a b c d e

2

a b c d e

3

a b c d e

4

a b c d e

5

a b c d e

6

a b c d e

7

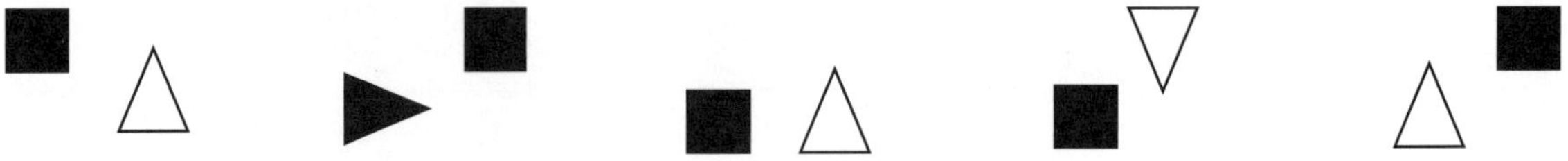

a b c d e

8

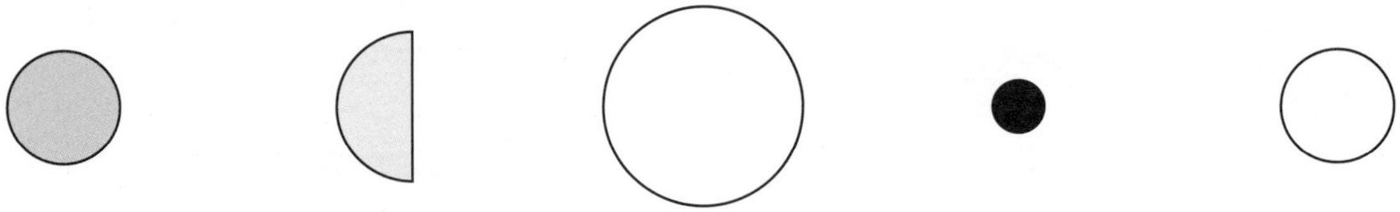

a b c d e

9

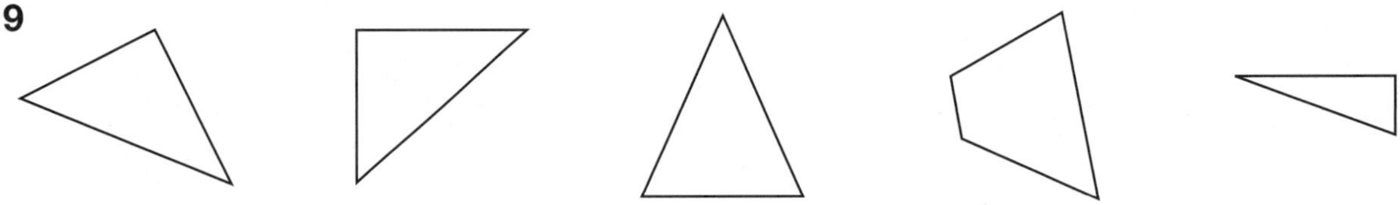

a b c d e

10

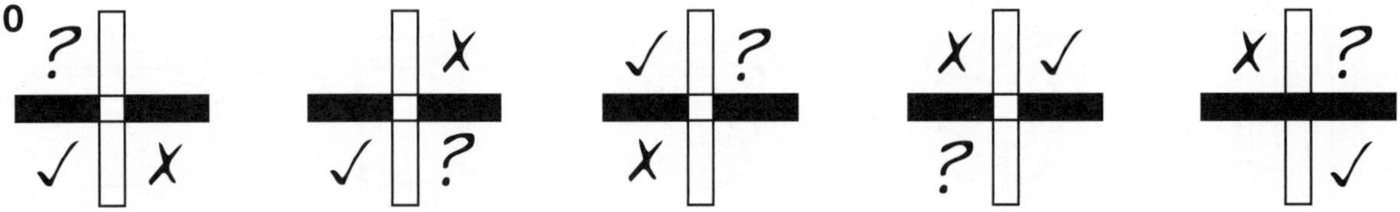

a b c d e

11

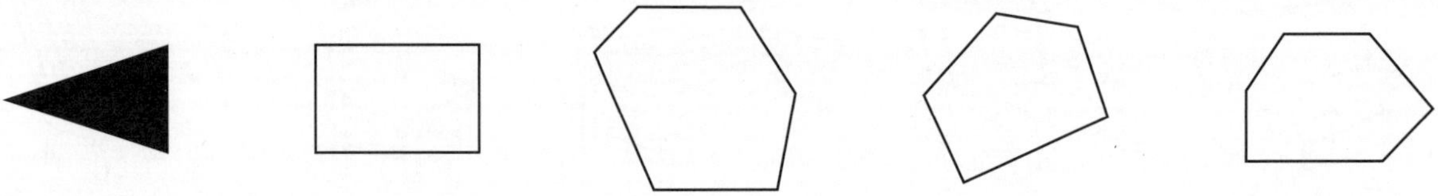

a b c d e

12

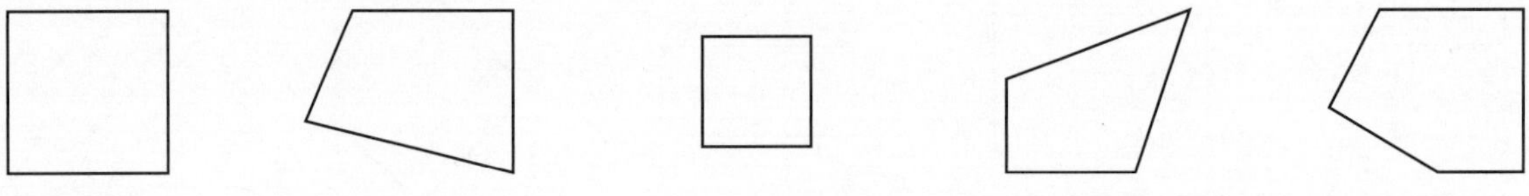

a b c d e

Which one comes next? Circle the letter.

Example

?

a b c d e

13

?

a b c d e

14

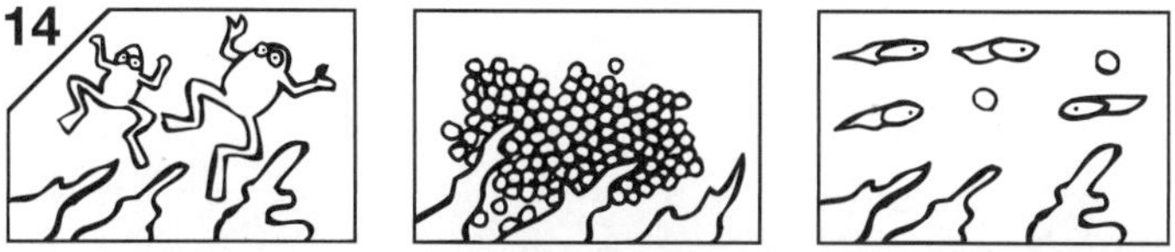

?

a b c d e

15

?

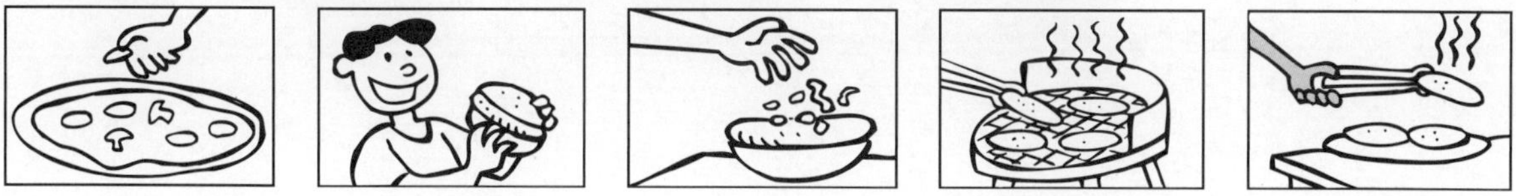

a b c d e

16

?

a **b** **c** **d** **e**

17

?

a **b** **c** **d** **e**

18

?

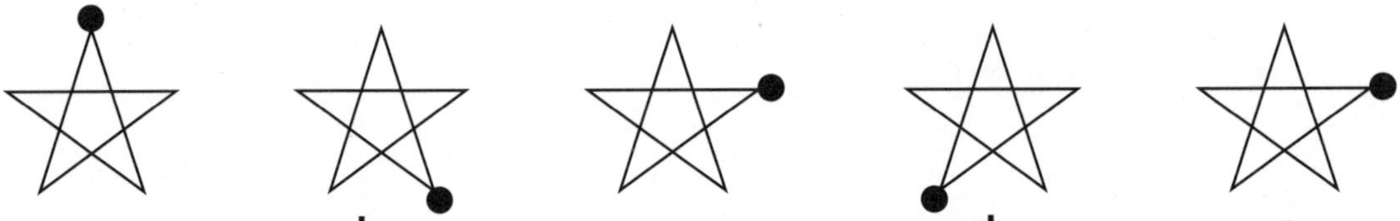

a **b** **c** **d** **e**

19

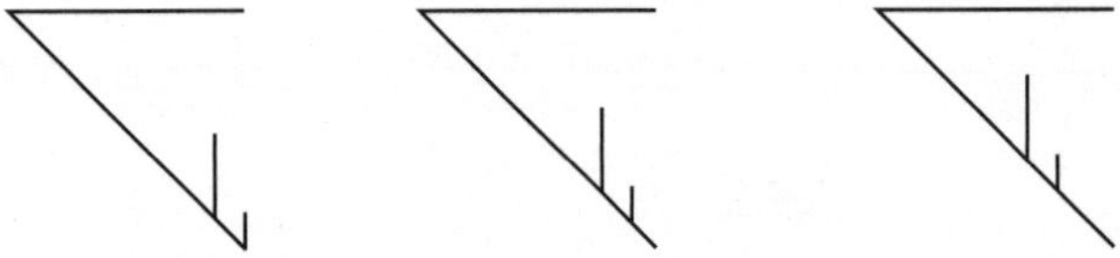

?

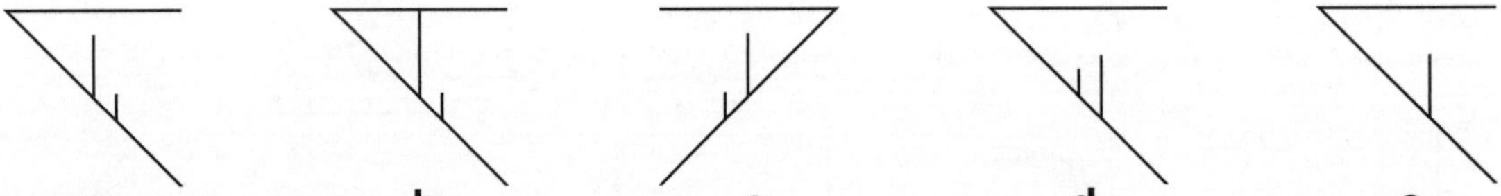

a **b** **c** **d** **e**

20

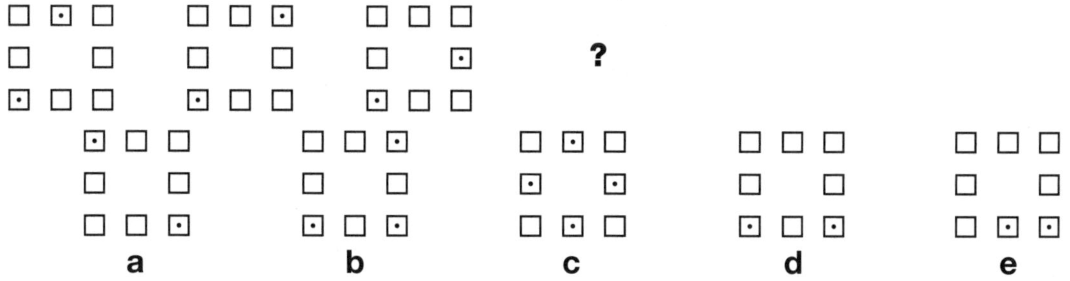

21

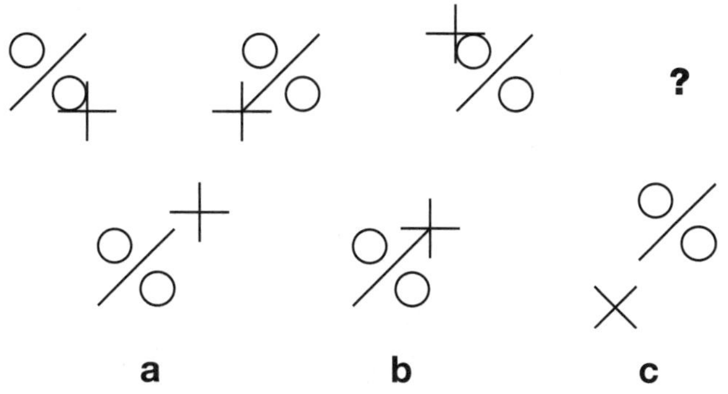

22

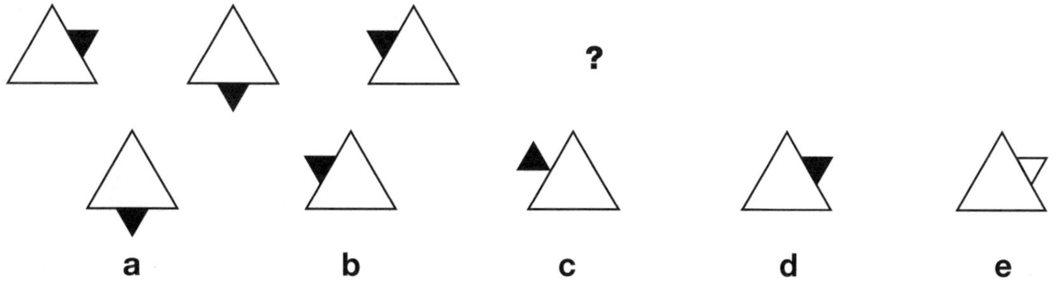

23

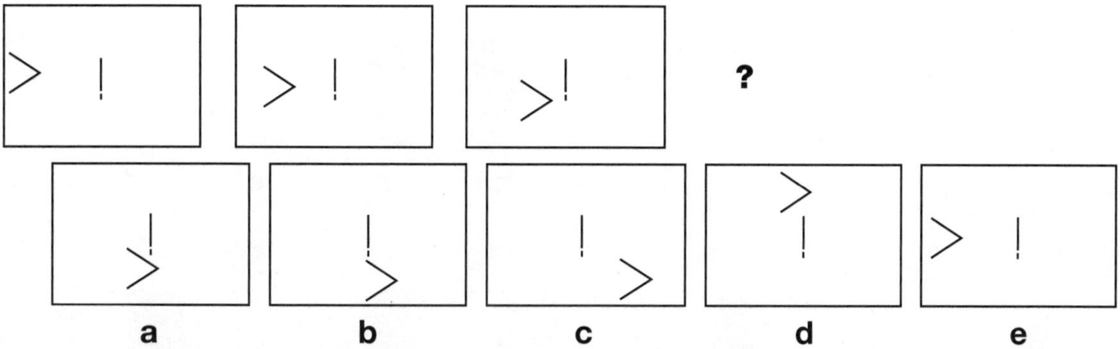

24

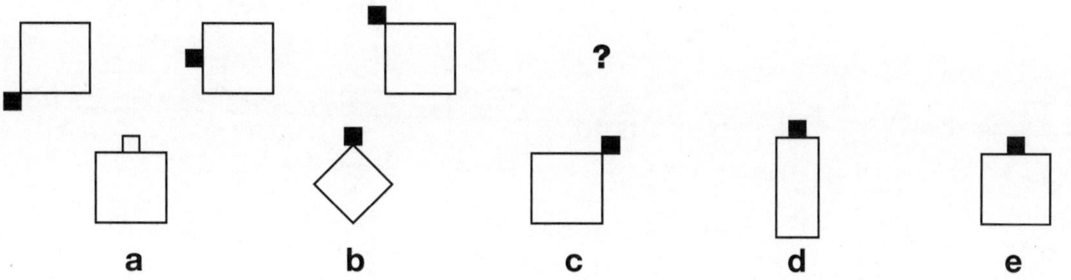

Which shape or pattern on the right completes the second pair in the same way as the first pair? Circle the letter.

Example

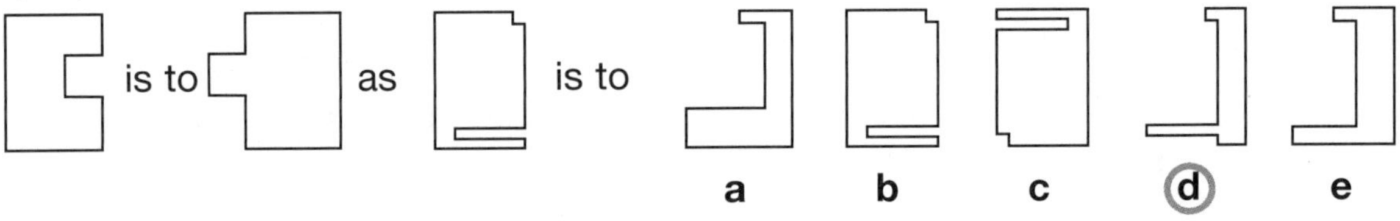

25

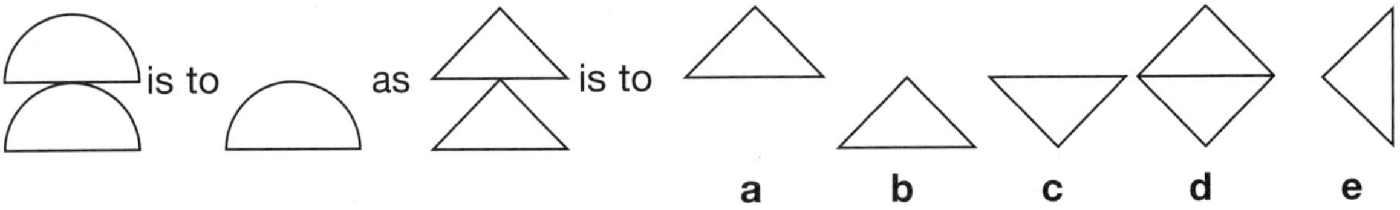

26

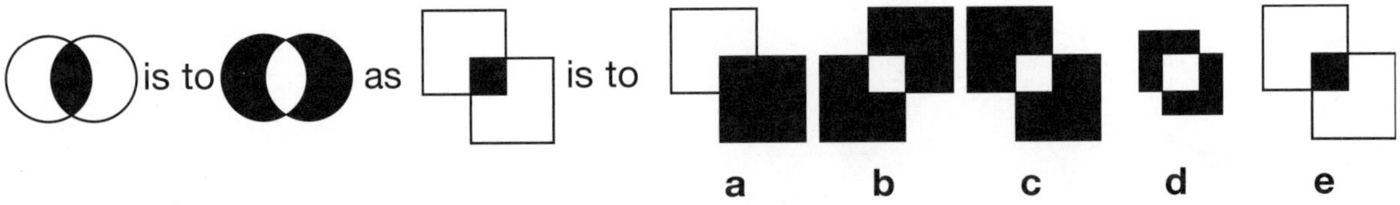

27

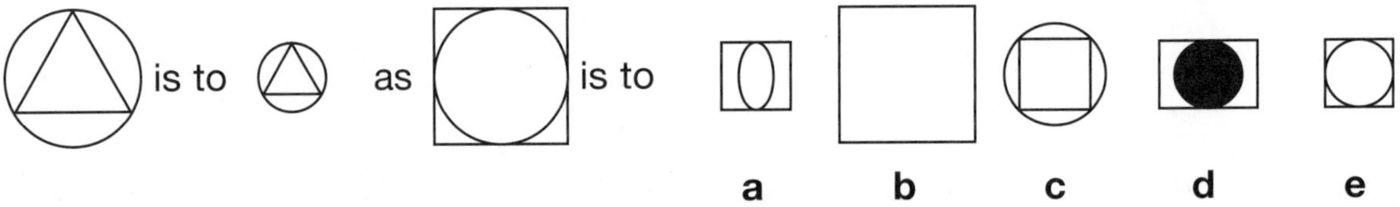

28

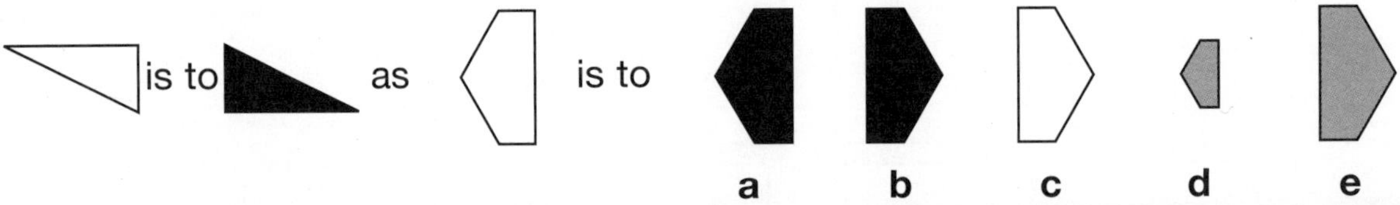

29

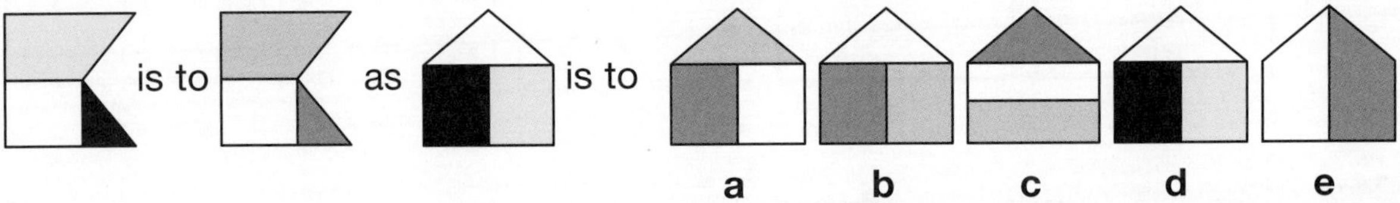

30

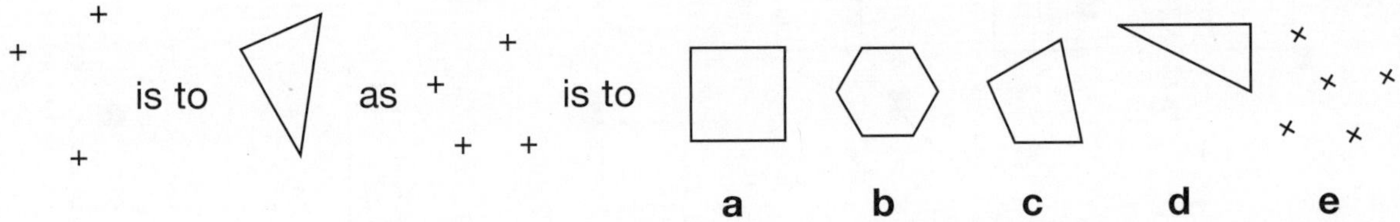

31

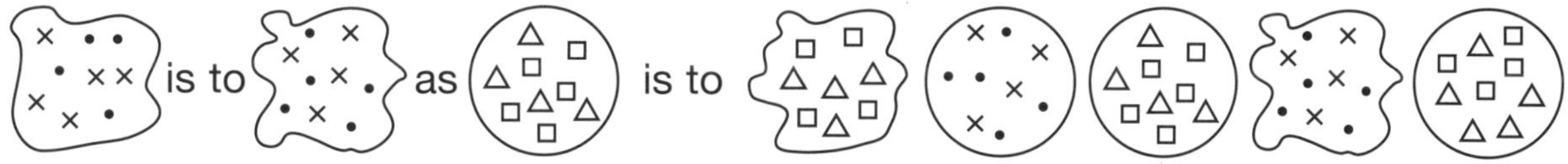

a b c d e

32

a b c d e

33

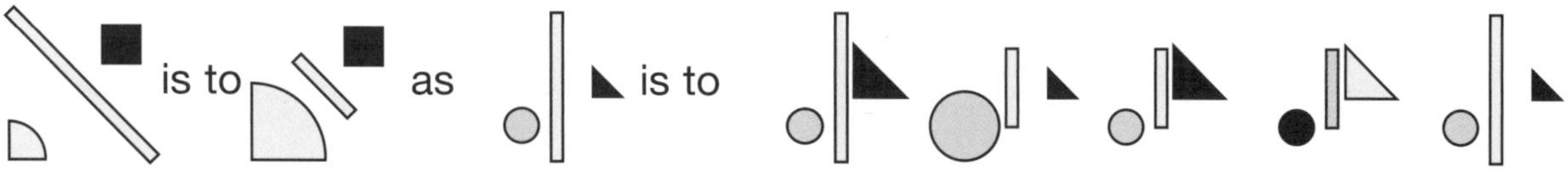

a b c d e

34

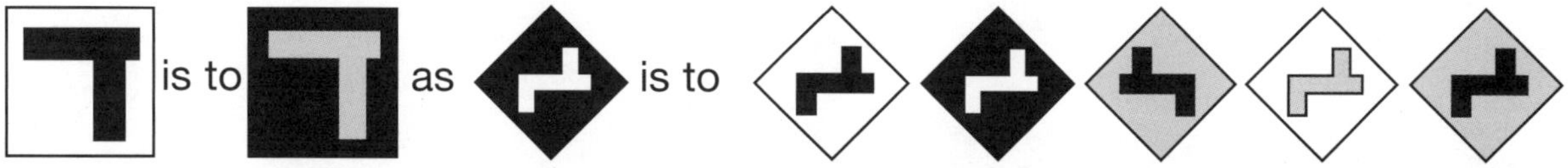

a b c d e

35

a b c d e

36

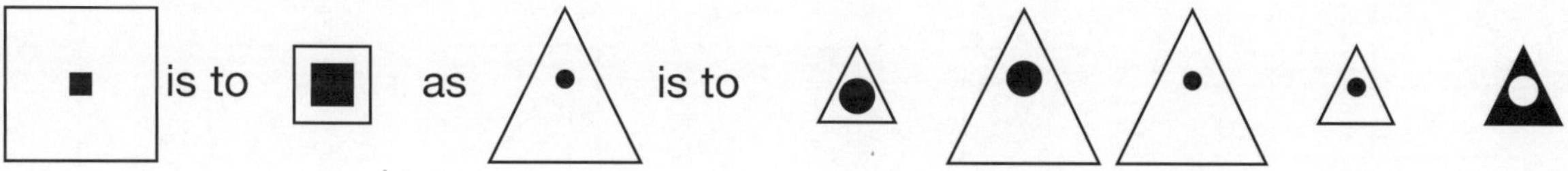

a b c d e

Which shape or pattern completes the larger square? Circle the letter.

Example

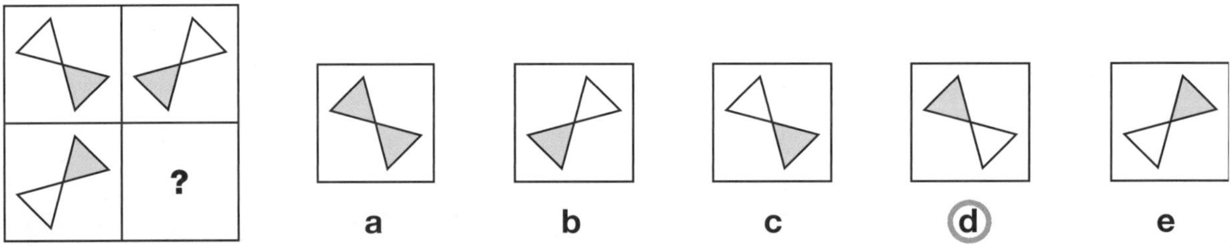

37

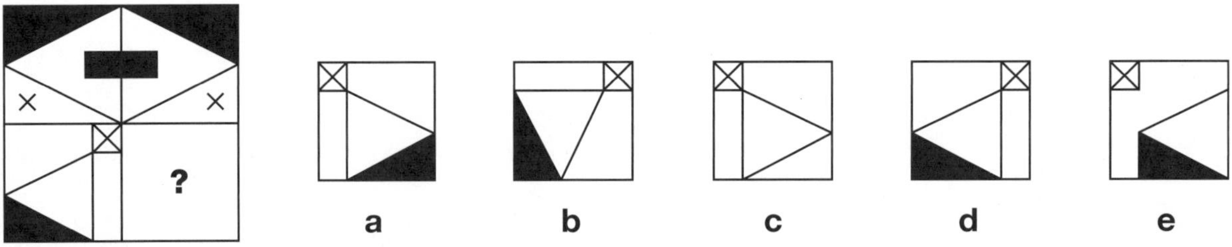

38

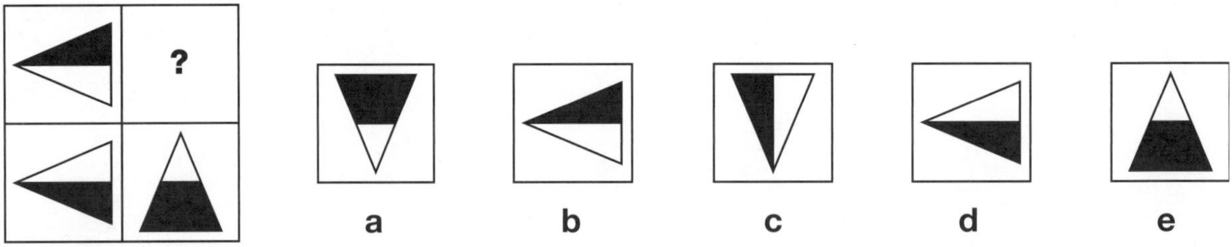

39

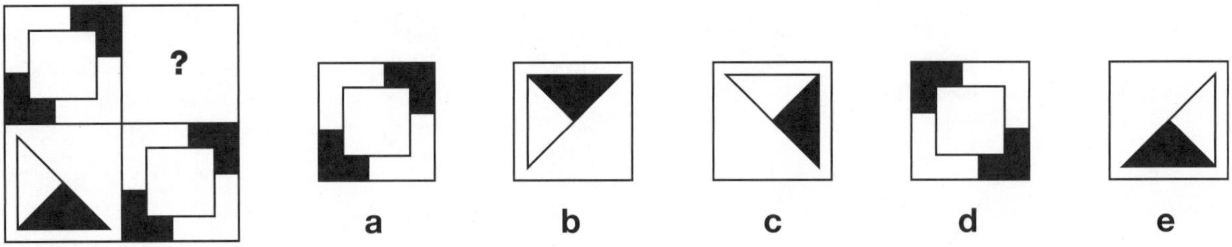

40

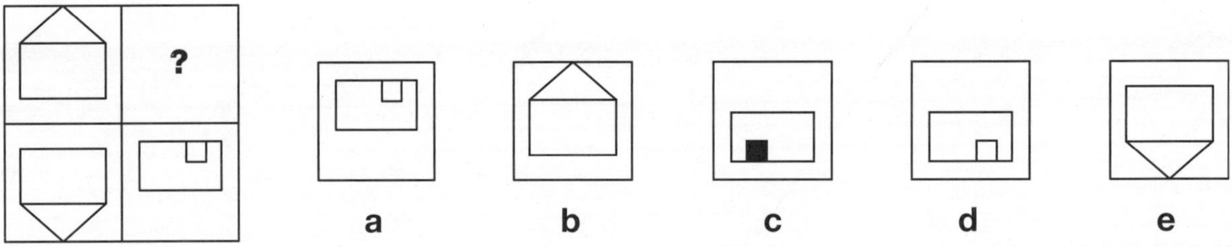

41

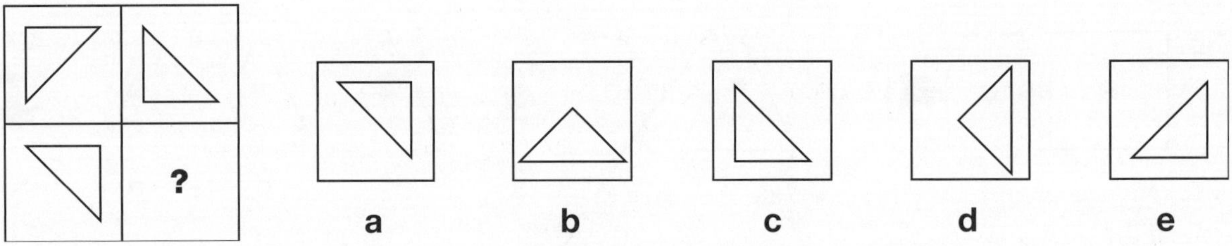

42

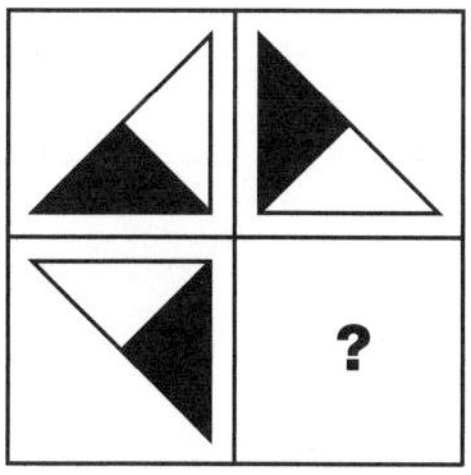

a

b

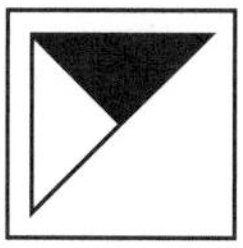

c

d

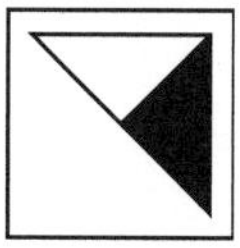

e

Which code matches the shape or pattern given at the end of each line?
Circle the letter.

Example

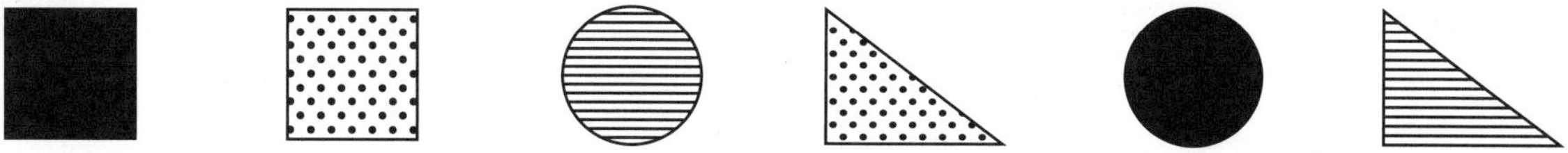

AX AY BZ CY BX **?**

a BZ **b** AZ **c** CX **d** BY **e** CZ

43

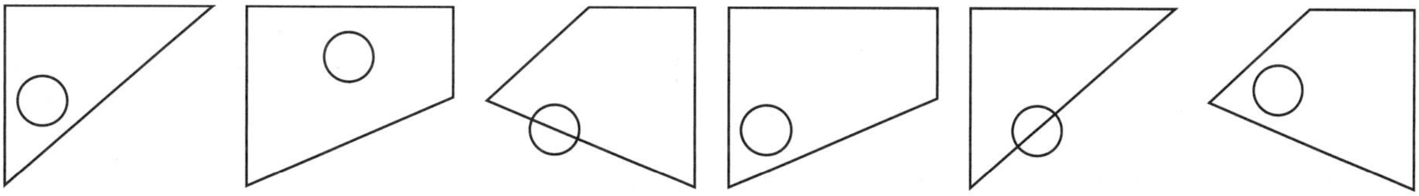

AJ BK CL BJ AL **?**

a BL **b** AK **c** CJ **d** CK **e** BK

44

DN EO DM FO EN **?**

a FN **b** EM **c** EO **d** DO **e** FM

45

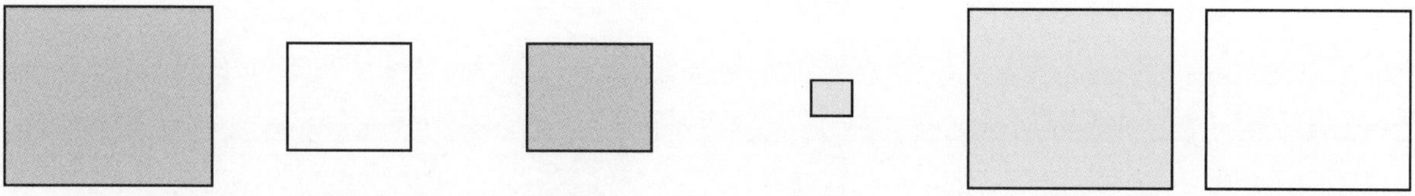

FR GS GR HT FT **?**

a GT **b** HR **c** HS **d** FT **e** FS

46

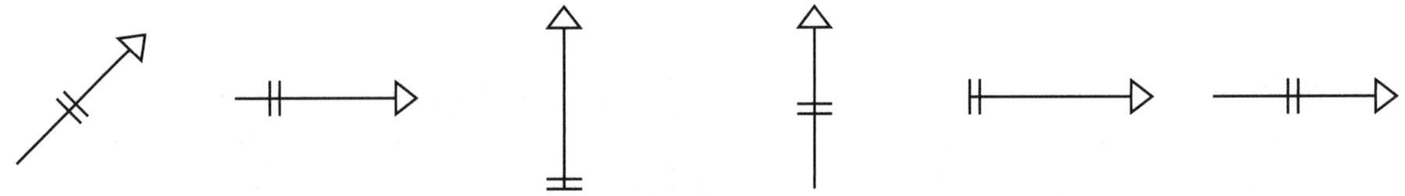

XP YQ ZR ZP YR ?

a ZQ **b** XQ **c** ZR **d** YP **e** XR

47

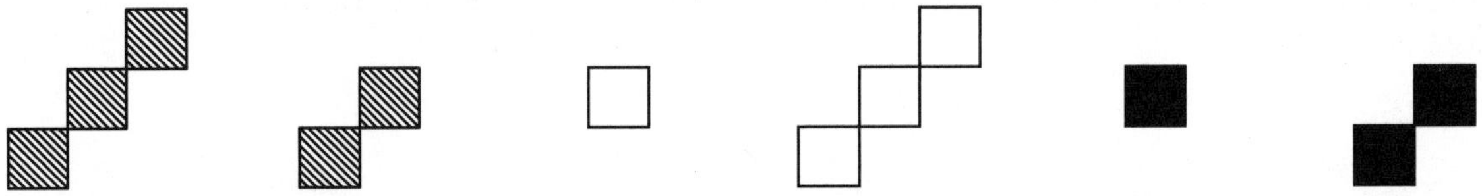

UL WL VM UM VN ?

a VN **b** WM **c** UL **d** WN **e** UN

48

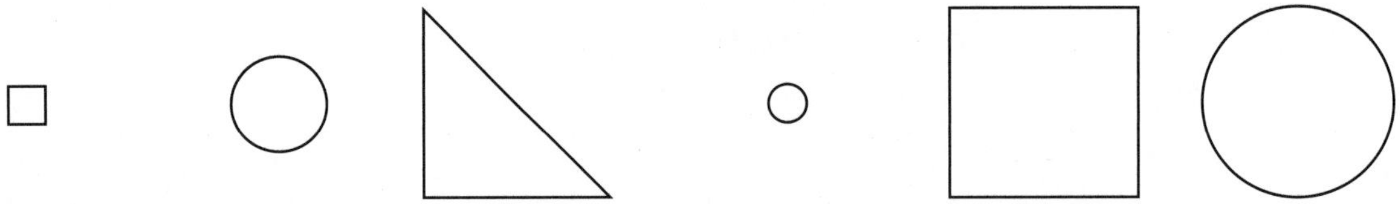

GA HB IC HA GC ?

a GB **b** IB **c** HC **d** HB **e** IA

Now go to the Progress Chart to record your score! Total 48

Paper 5

Which is the odd one out? Circle the letter.

Example

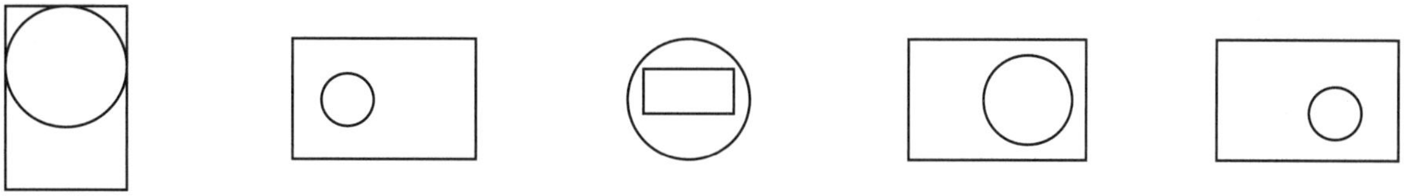

a b (c) d e

1

a b c d e

2

a b c d e

3

a b c d e

4

a b c d e

5

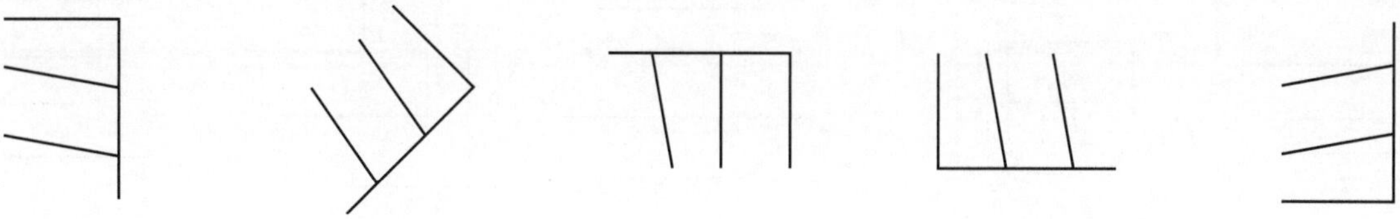

a b c d e

6

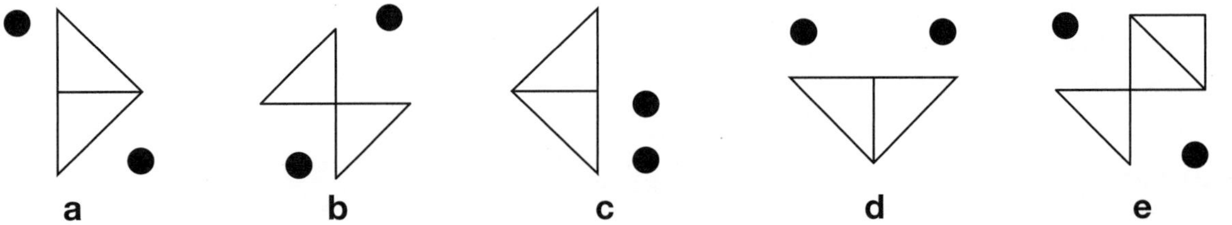

7

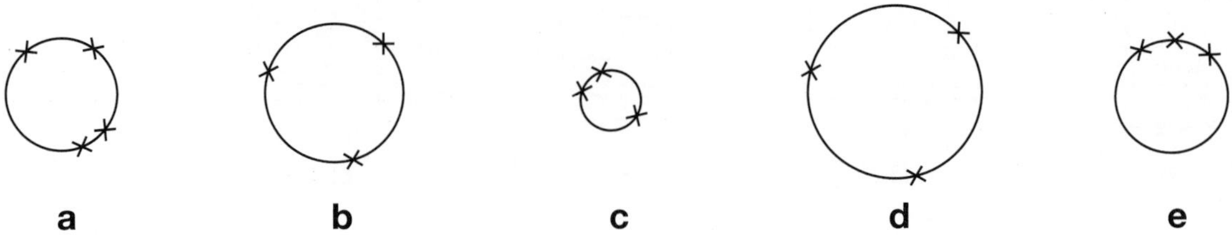

8

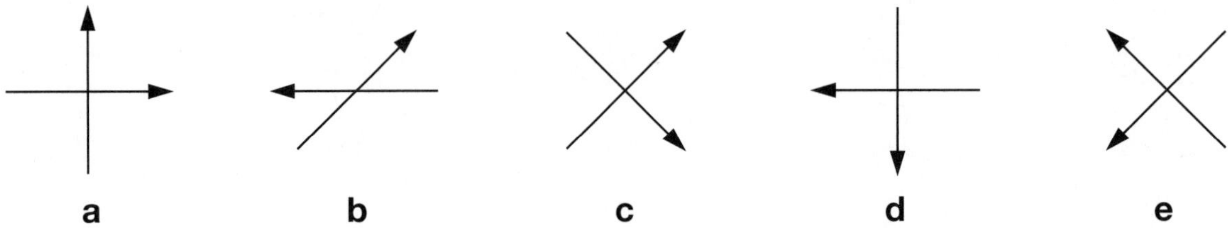

9

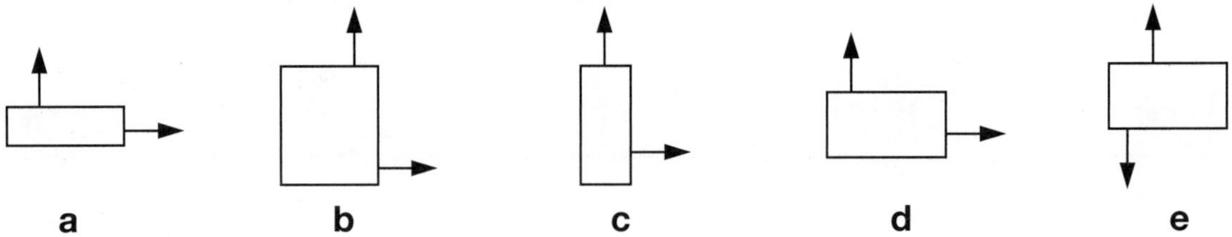

10

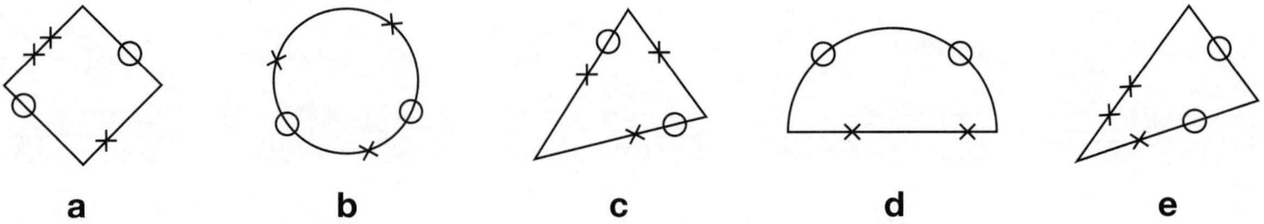

11

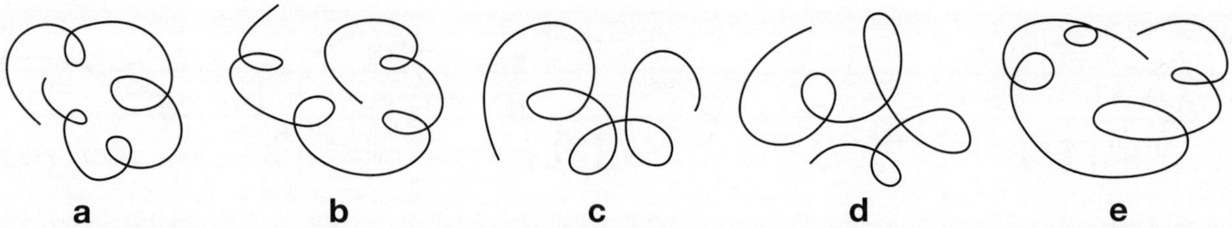

12

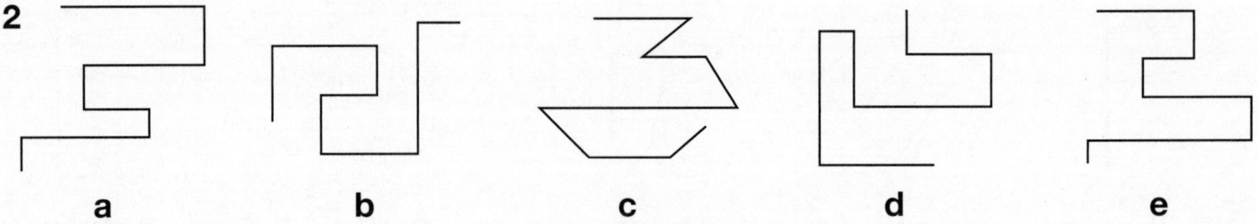

Which one comes next? Circle the letter.

Example

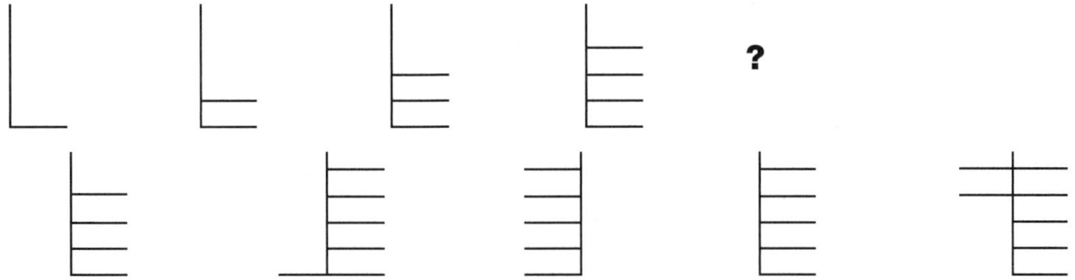

a b c (d) e

13

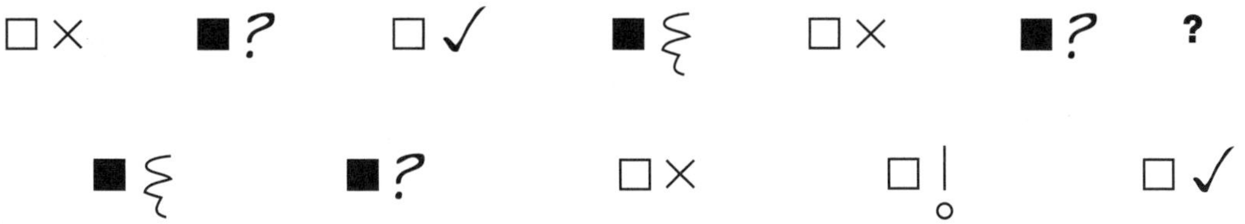

a b c d e

14

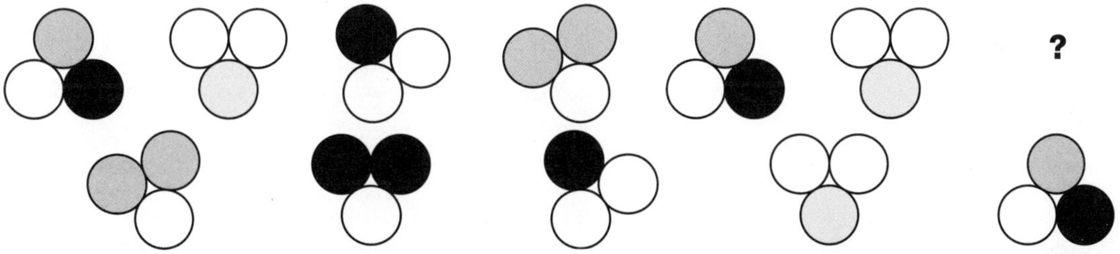

a b c d e

15

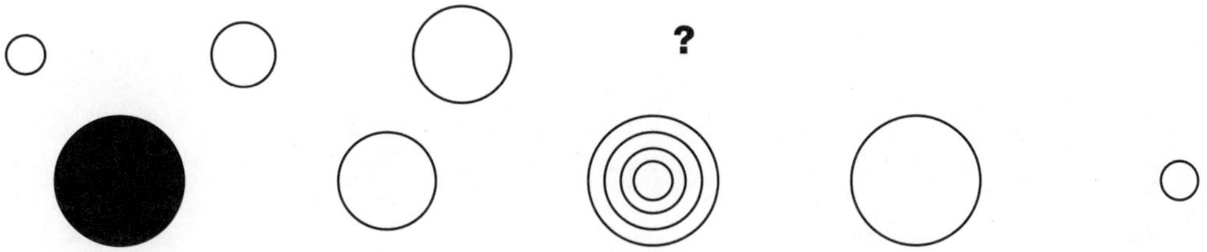

a b c d e

16

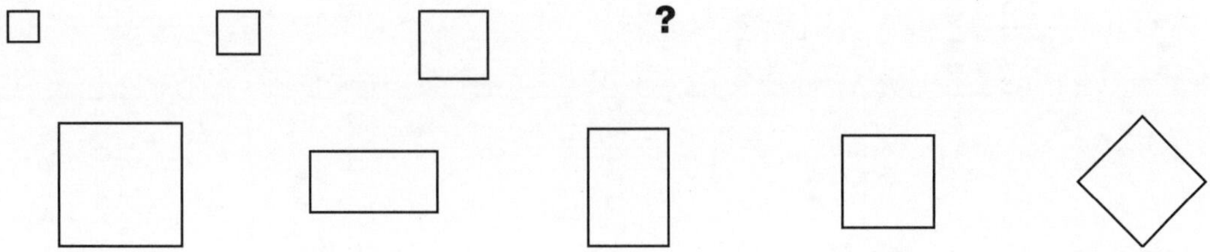

a b c d e

17

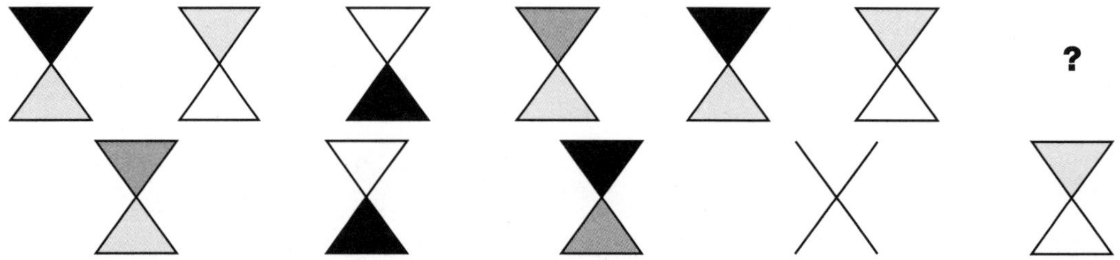

a b c d e

18

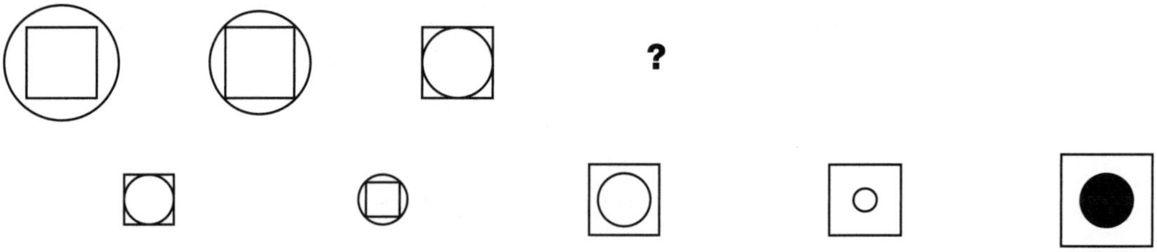

a b c d e

19

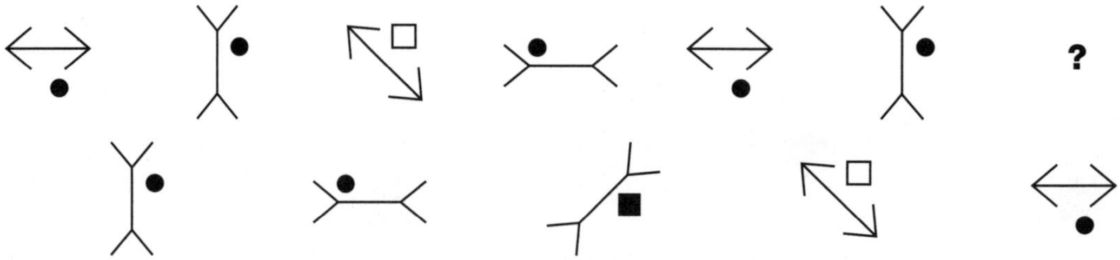

a b c d e

20

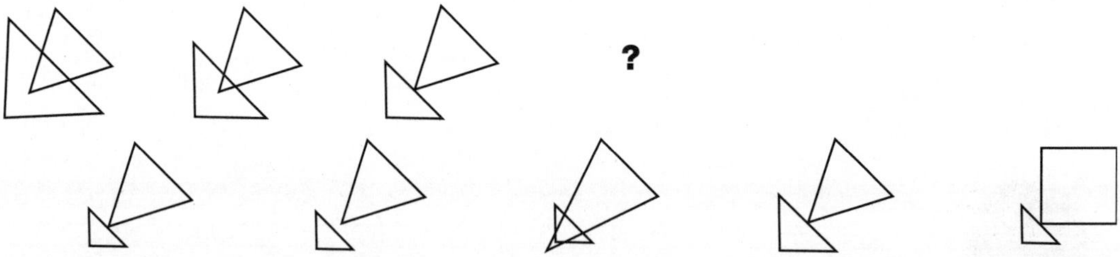

a b c d e

21

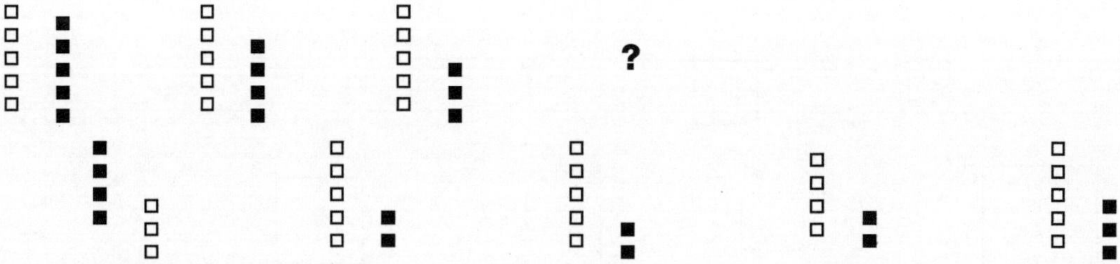

a b c d e

22

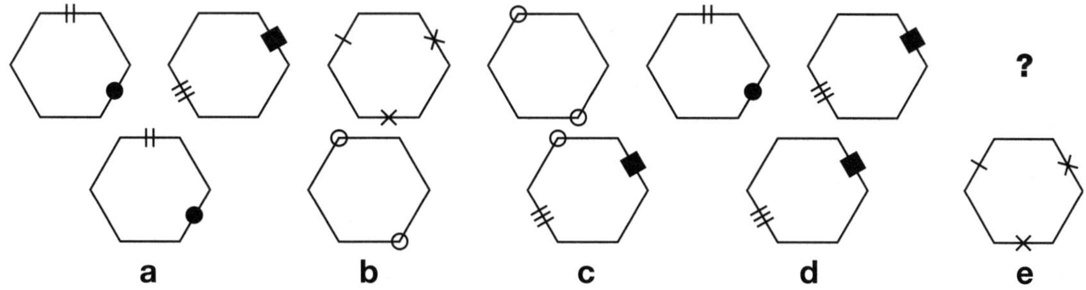

23

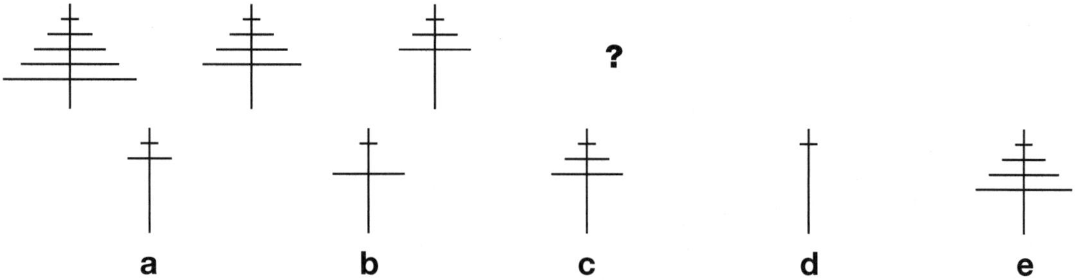

24

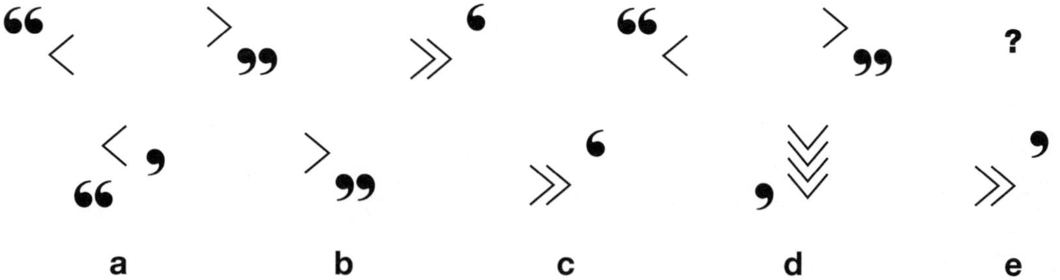

Which picture completes the second pair in the same way as the first pair?
Circle the letter.

Example

 is to  as  is to **?**

 **a**

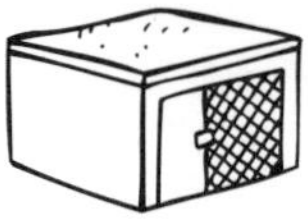 **b**

 **c**

 **d**

 **e**

25  is to  as  is to **?**

 **a**

 **b**

 **c**

 **d**

 **e**

26  is to 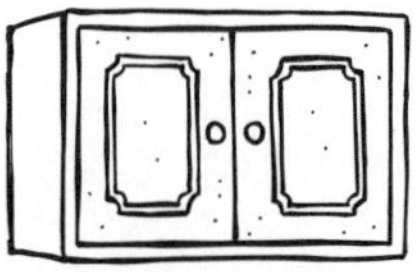 as  is to **?**

 **a**

 **b**

 **c**

 **d**

 **e**

27 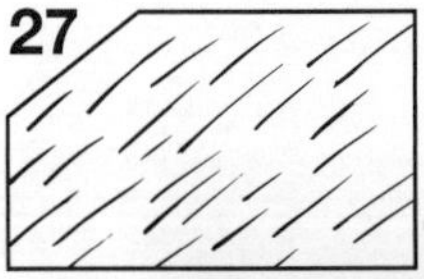 is to  as 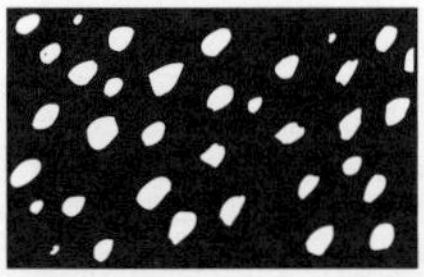 is to **?**

 **a**

 **b**

 **c**

 **d**

 **e**

28  is to  as  is to **?**

 **a**  **b**  **c**  **d**  **e**

29  is to  as  is to **?**

 **a**  **b**  **c**  **d**  **e**

30  is to  as  is to **?**

 **a**  **b**  **c**  **d**  **e**

31 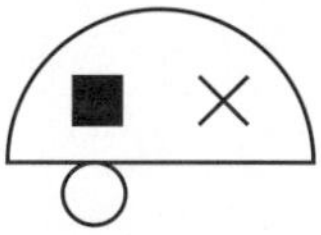 is to 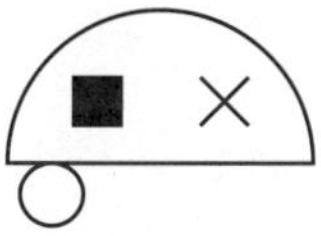 as 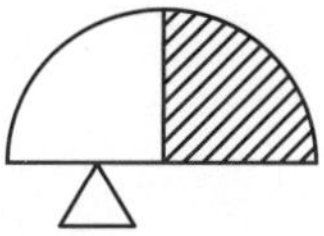 is to **?**

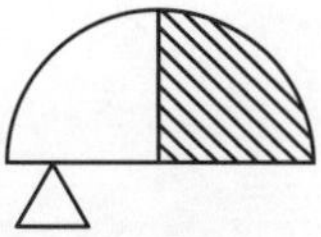 **a** 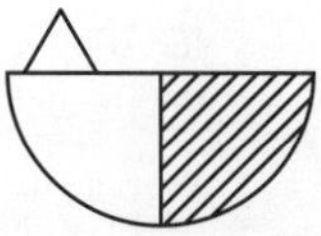 **b** 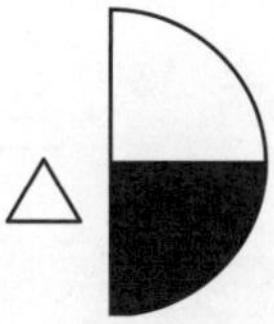 **c** 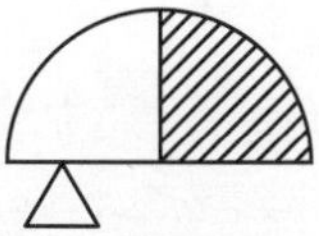 **d** 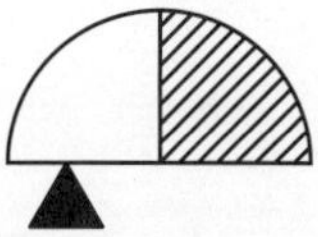 **e**

32

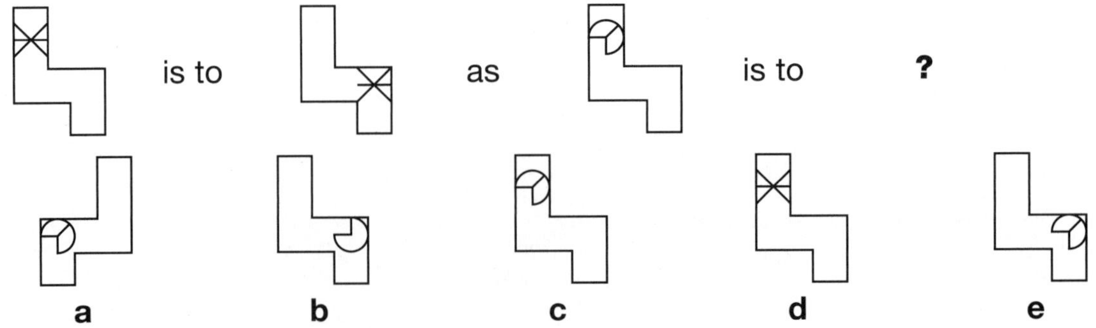
is to
as
is to
?
a
b
c
d
e

33

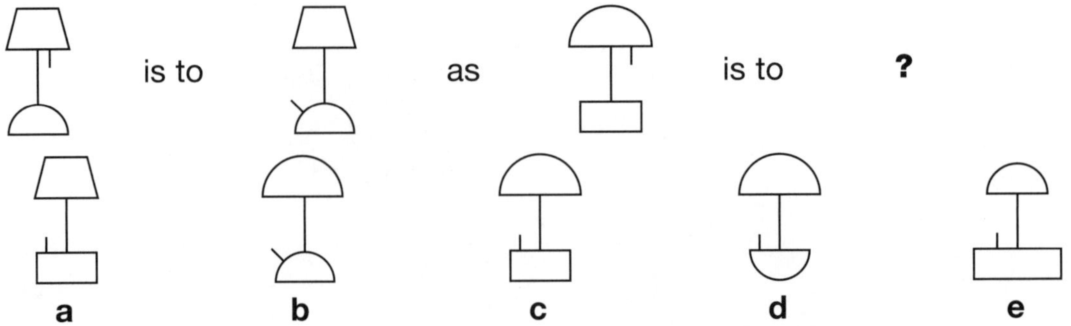
is to
as
is to
?
a
b
c
d
e

34

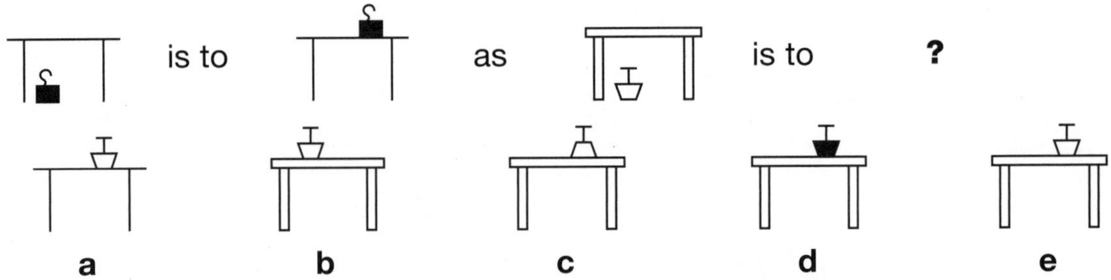
is to
as
is to
?
a
b
c
d
e

35

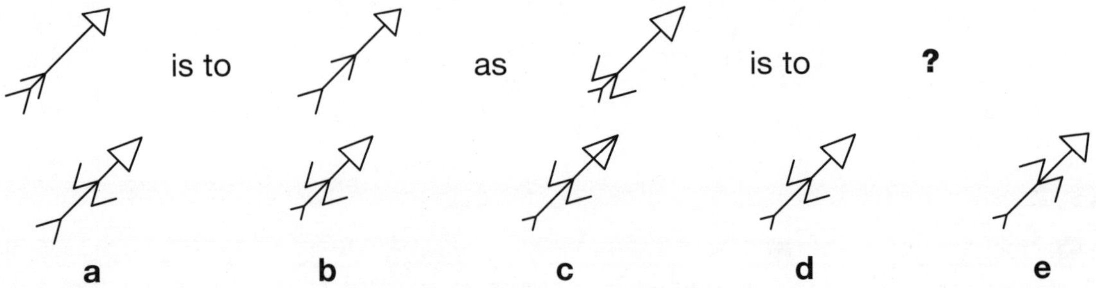
is to
as
is to
?
a
b
c
d
e

36

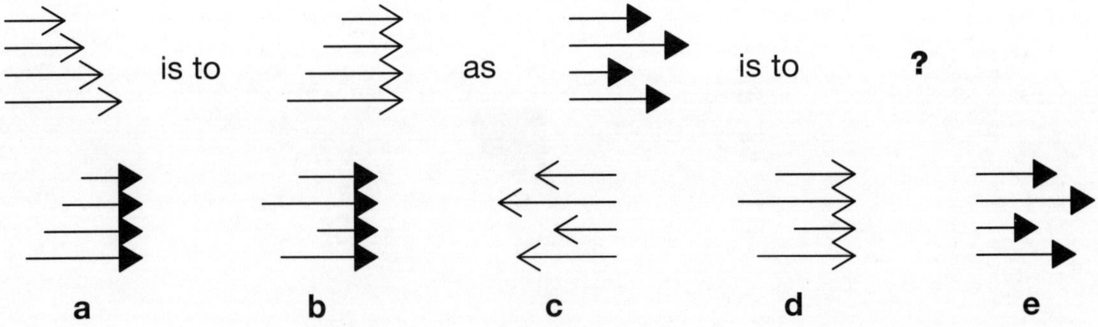
is to
as
is to
?
a
b
c
d
e

In which larger shape is the shape on the left hidden? Circle the letter.

Example

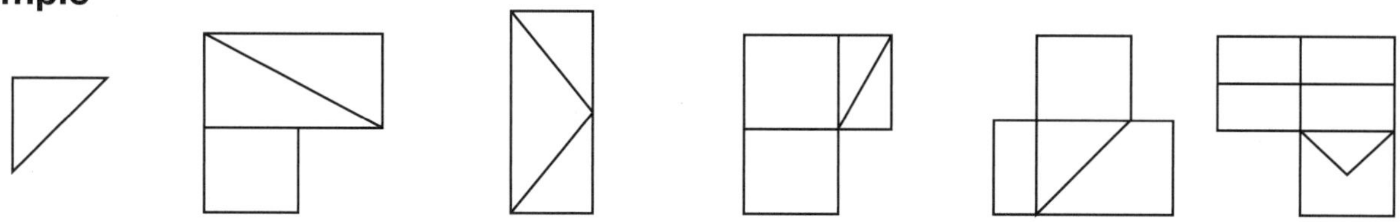

a b c d e

37

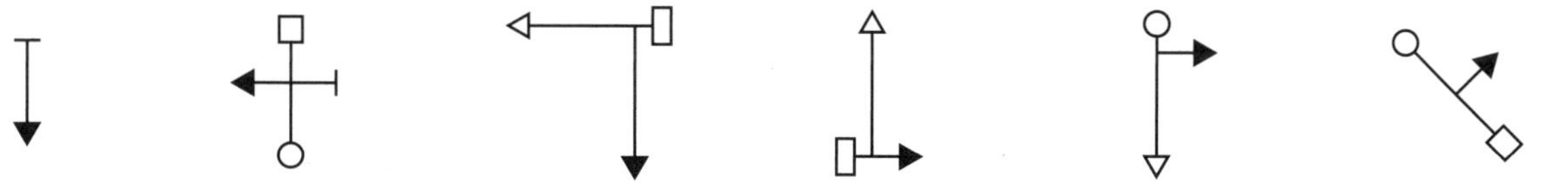

a b c d e

38

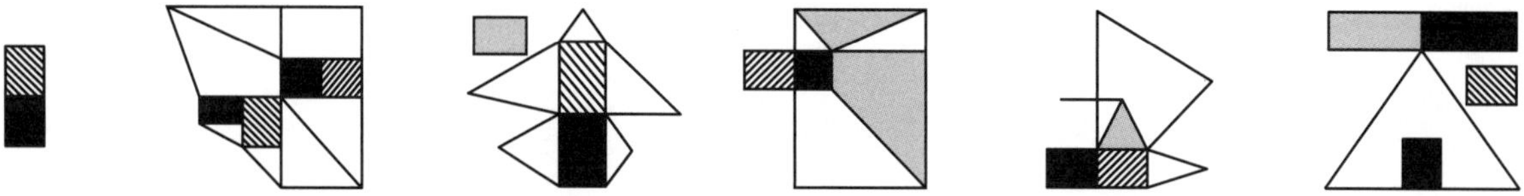

a b c d e

39

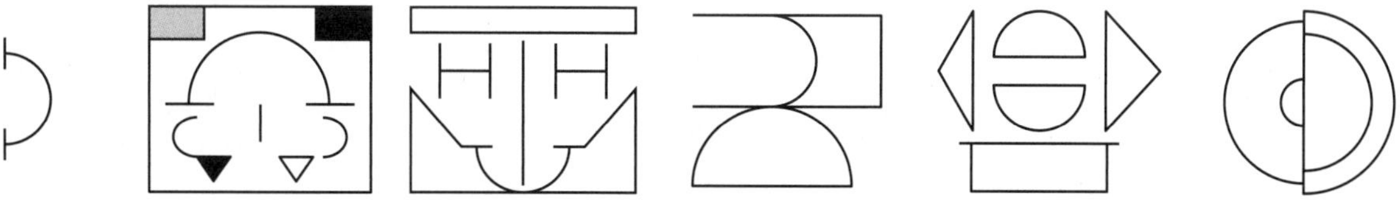

a b c d e

40

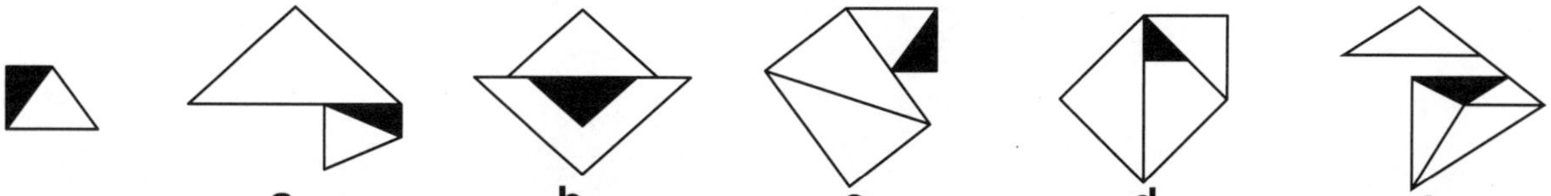

a b c d e

41

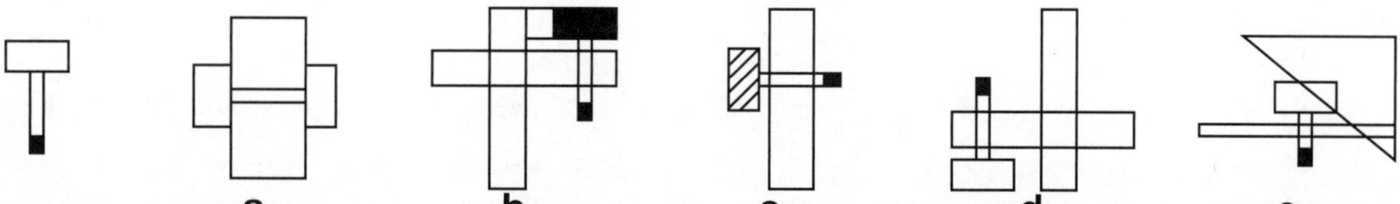

a b c d e

42

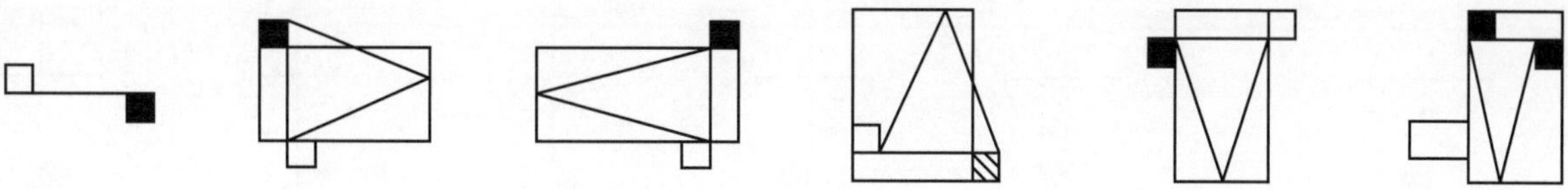

a b c d e

Which shape on the right is the reflection of the shape given on the left? Circle the letter.

Example

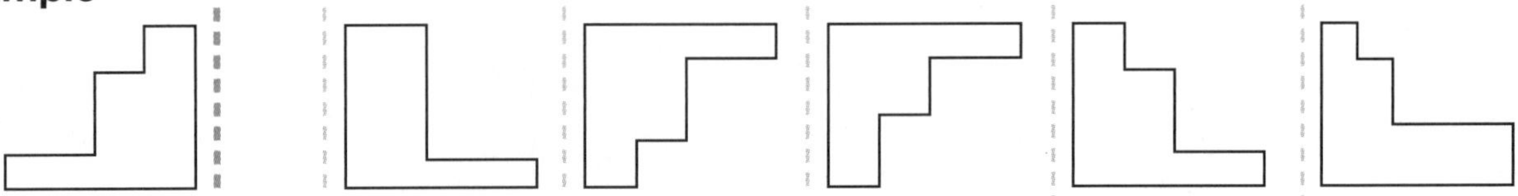

a b c (d) e

43

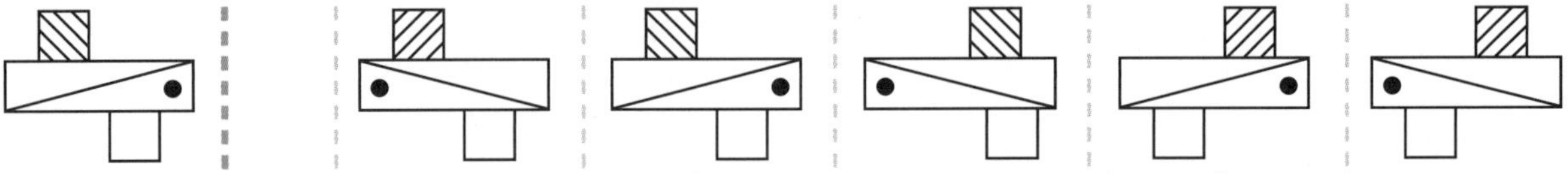

a b c d e

44

a b c d e

45

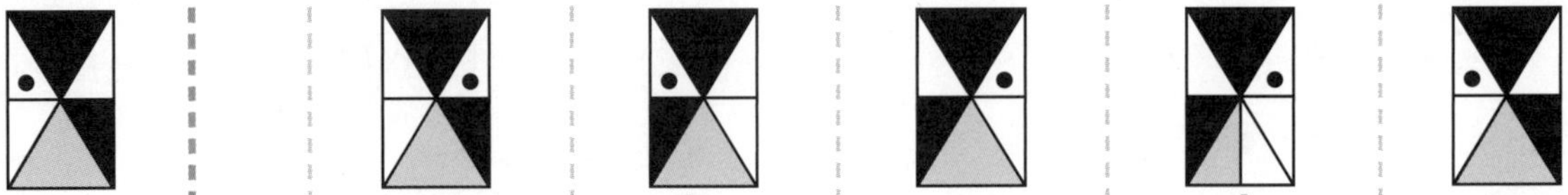

a b c d e

46

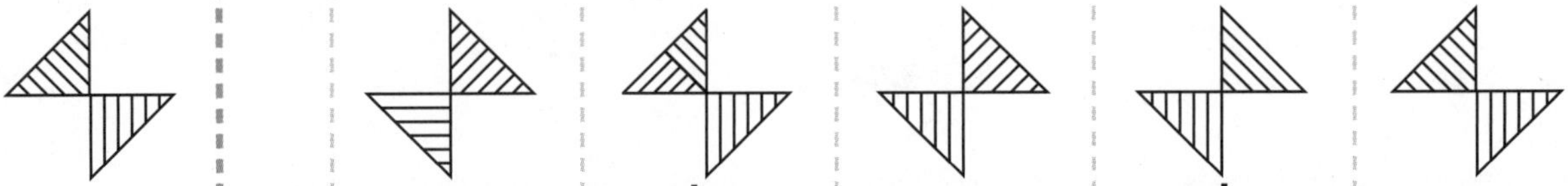

a b c d e

47

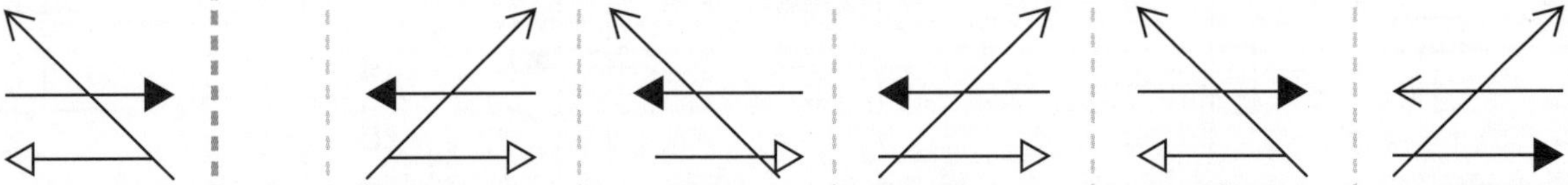

a b c d e

48

a b c d e

Paper 6

Which is the odd one out? Circle the letter.

Example

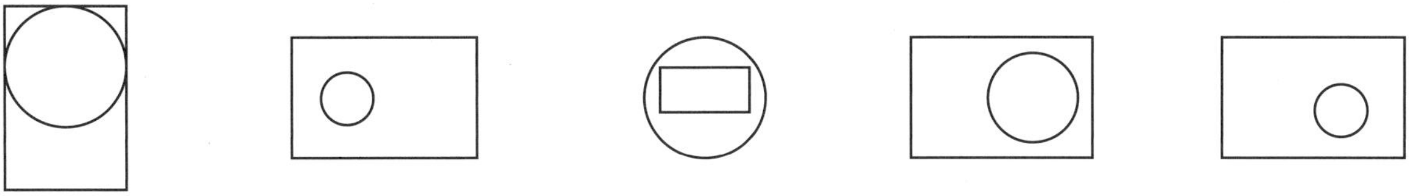

a b (c) d e

1

a b c d e

2

a b c d e

3

a b c d e

4

a b c d e

5

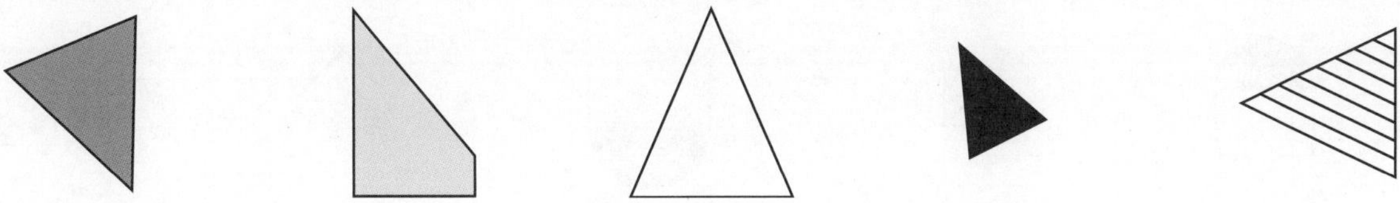

a b c d e

6

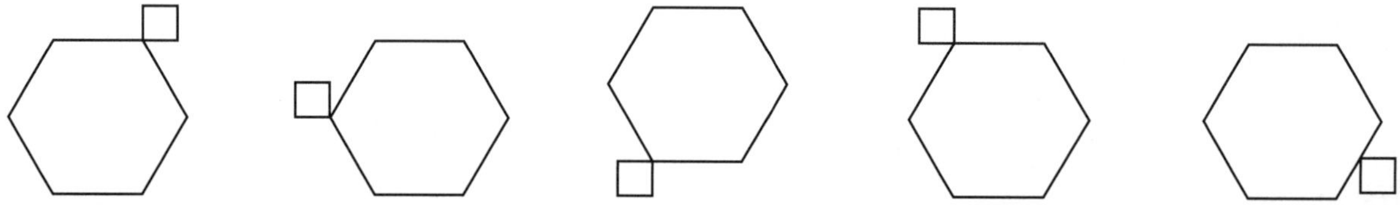

a b c d e

7

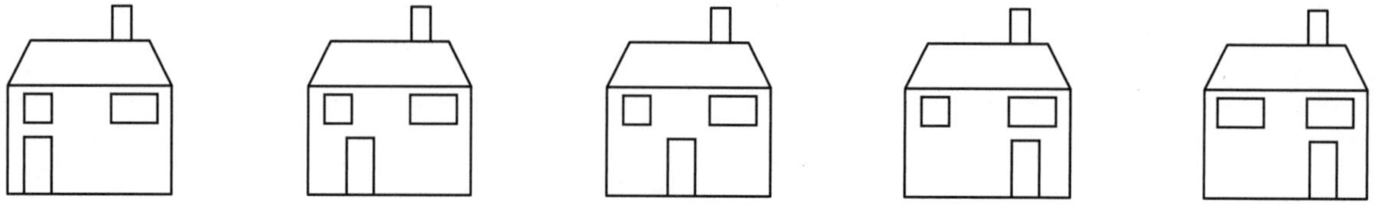

a b c d e

8

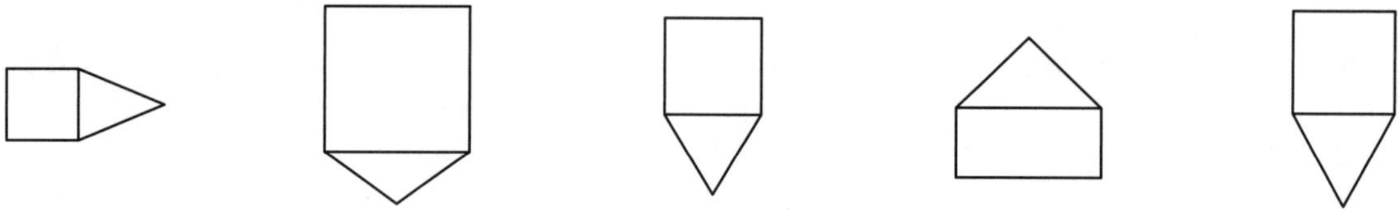

a b c d e

9

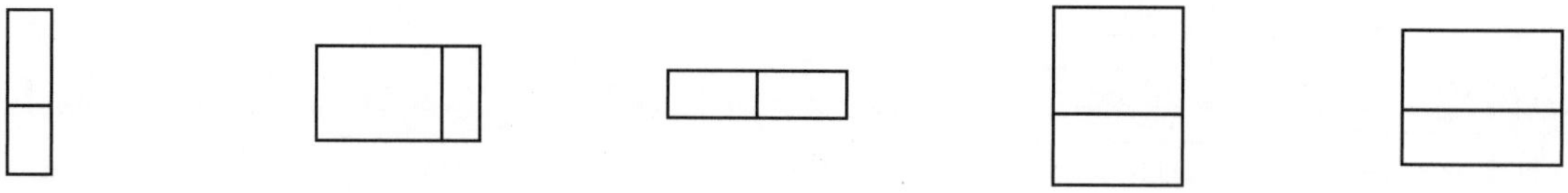

a b c d e

10

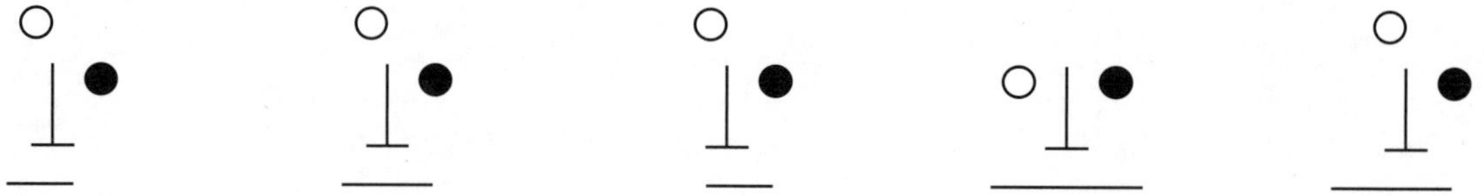

a b c d e

11

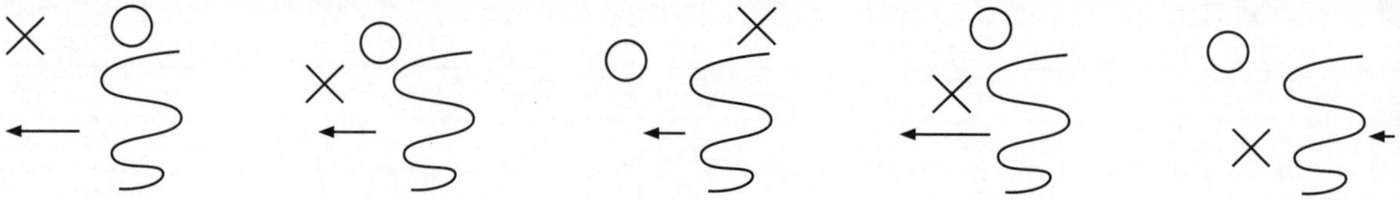

a b c d e

12

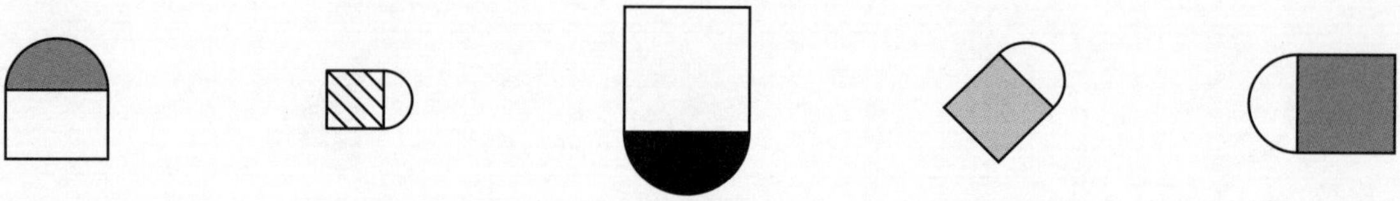

a b c d e

Which one comes next? Circle the letter.

Example

a b c d e

13

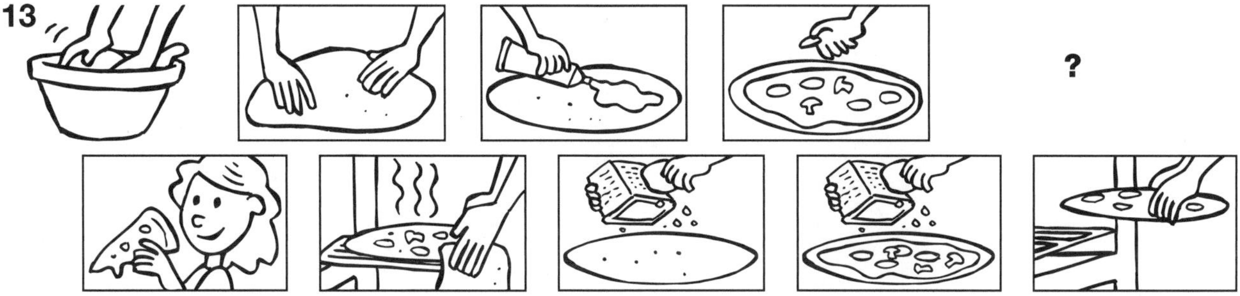

a b c d e

14

a b c d e

15

a b c d e

16

?

a b c d e

17

?

a b c d e

18

?

a b c d e

19

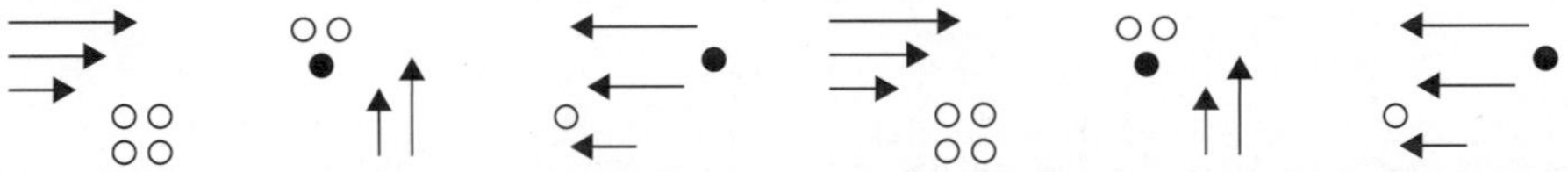

?

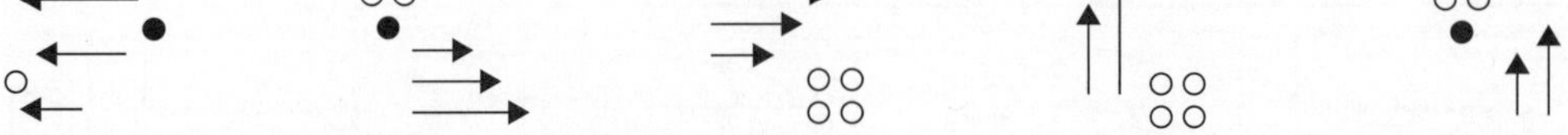

a b c d e

20

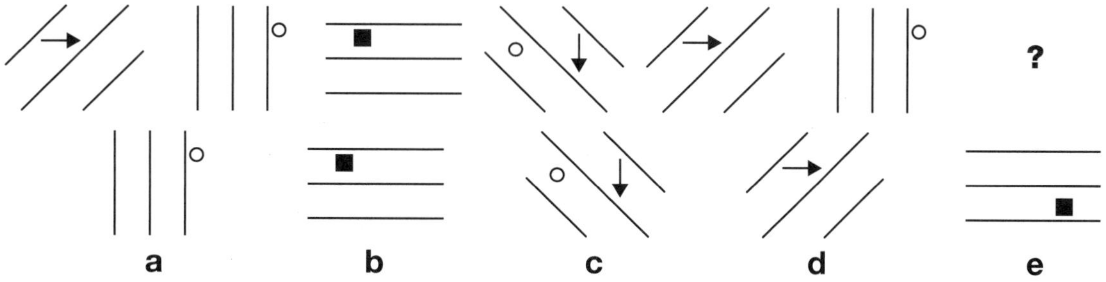

21

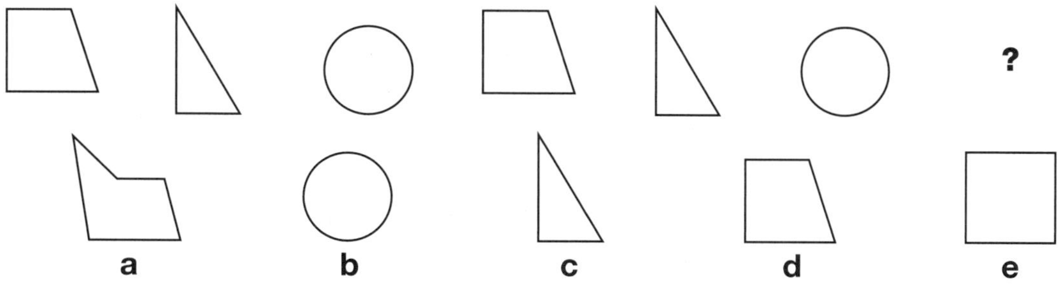

22

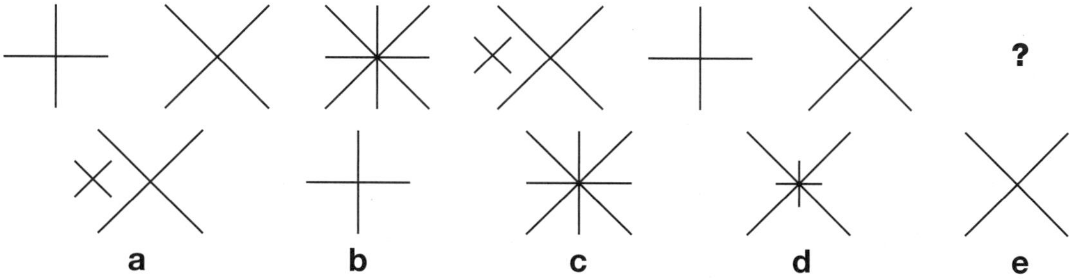

23

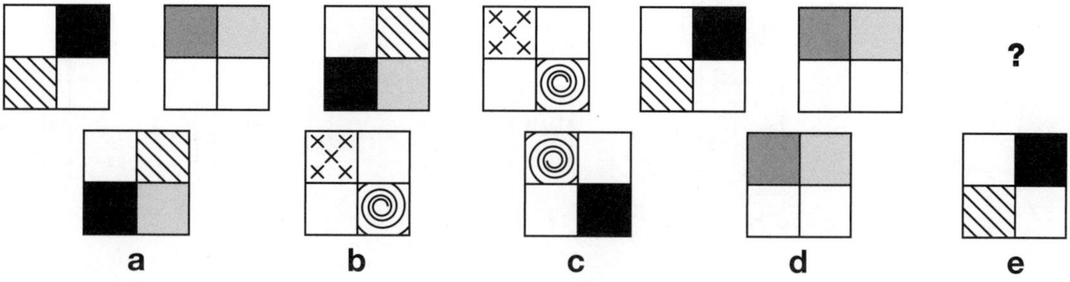

24

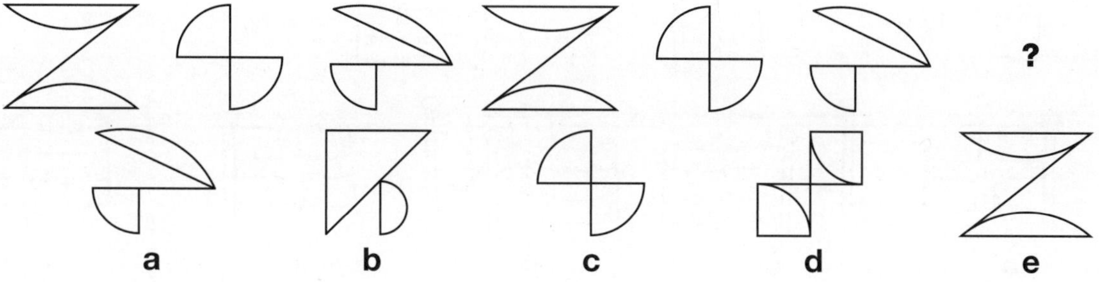

Which picture completes the second pair in the same way as the first pair? Circle the letter.

Example

 is to  as  is to **?**

 **a**
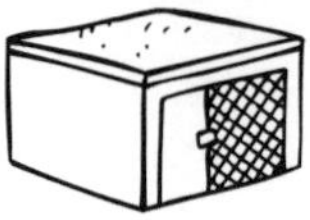 **b**
 **c**
 **d**
 **e**

25  is to  as  is to **?**

 **a**
 **b**
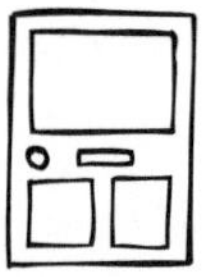 **c**
 **d**
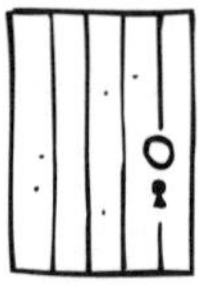 **e**

26  is to  as  is to **?**

 **a**
 **b**
 **c**
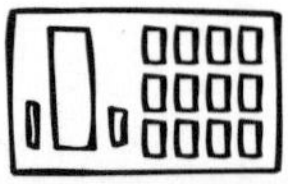 **d**
 **e**

27 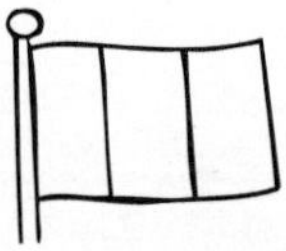 is to 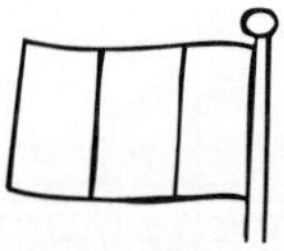 as 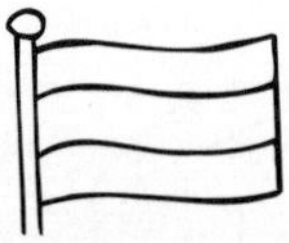 is to **?**

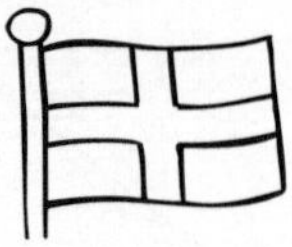 **a**
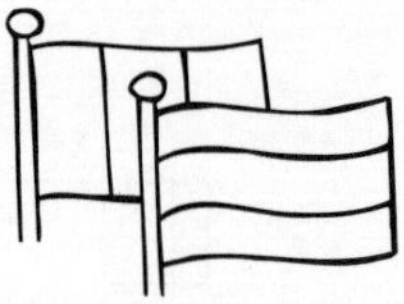 **b**
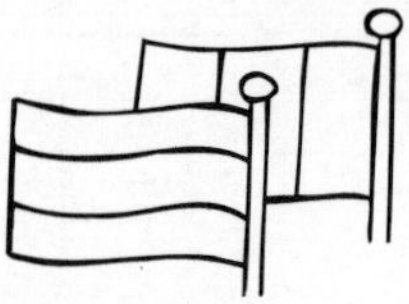 **c**
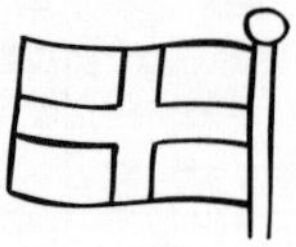 **d**
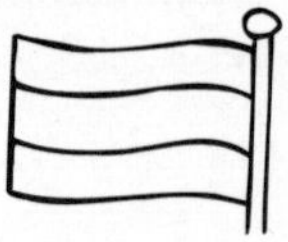 **e**

28

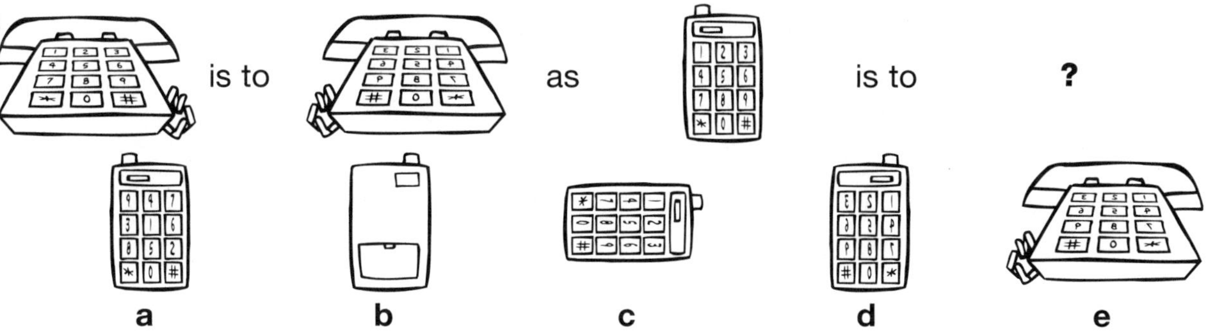
is to
as
is to
?
a
b
c
d
e

29

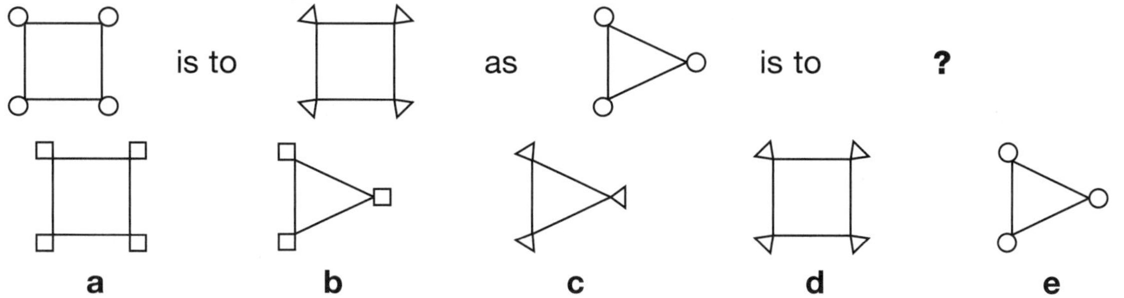
is to
as
is to
?
a
b
c
d
e

30

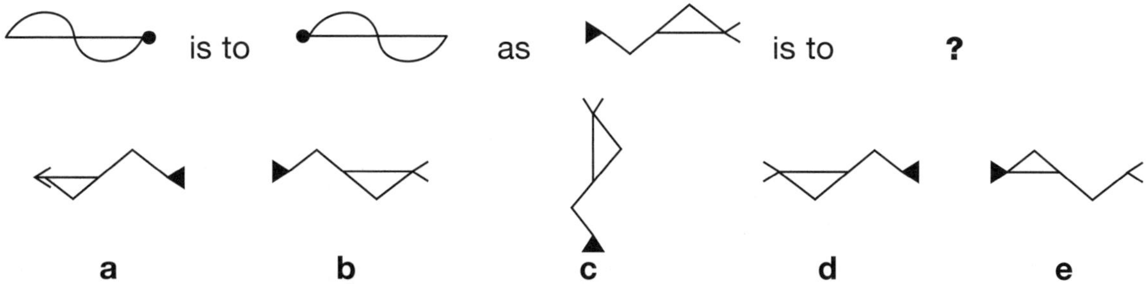
is to
as
is to
?
a
b
c
d
e

31

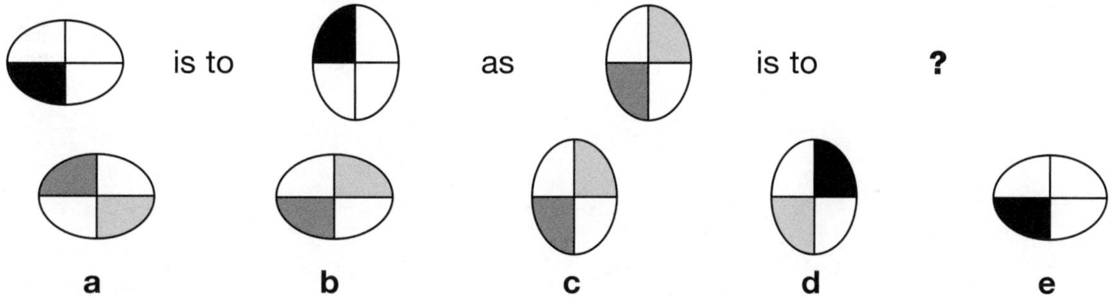
is to
as
is to
?
a
b
c
d
e

32

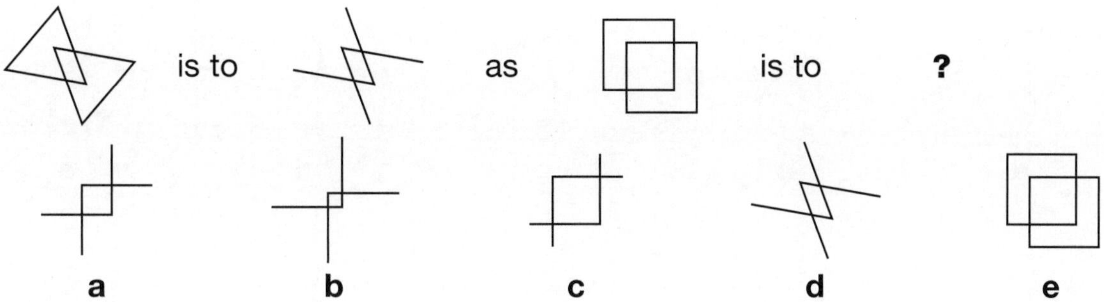
is to
as
is to
?
a
b
c
d
e

33
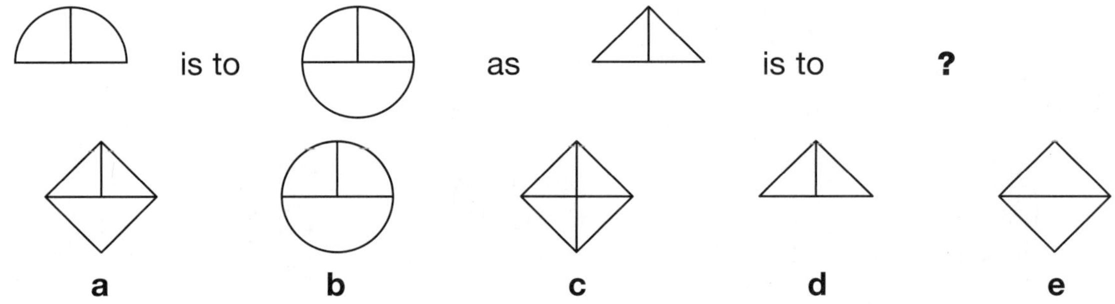
is to
as
is to
?
a
b
c
d
e

34
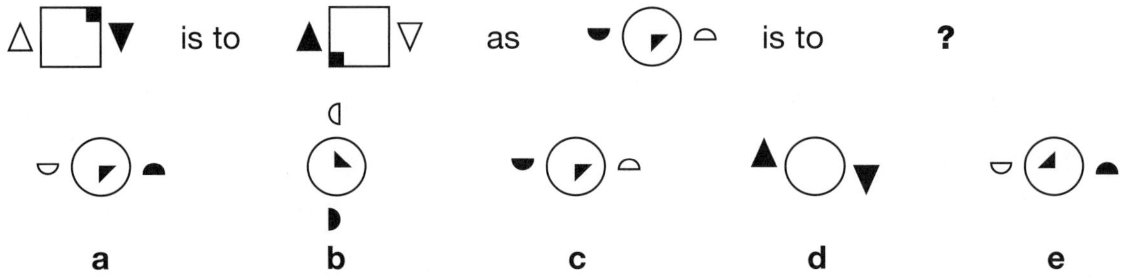
is to
as
is to
?
a
b
c
d
e

35
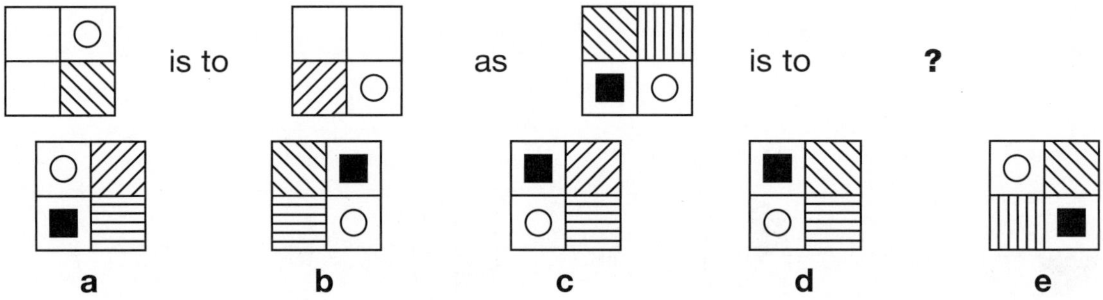
is to
as
is to
?
a
b
c
d
e

36
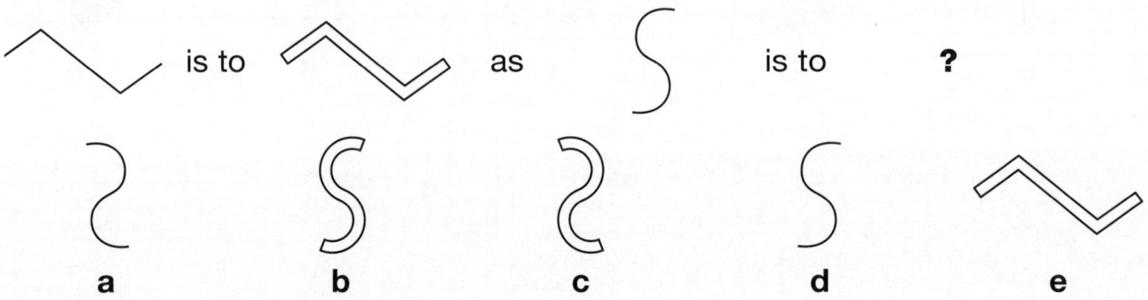
is to
as
is to
?
a
b
c
d
e

Which shape or pattern completes the larger square? Circle the letter.

Example

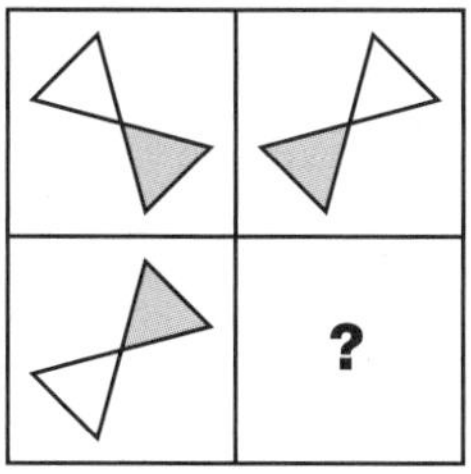

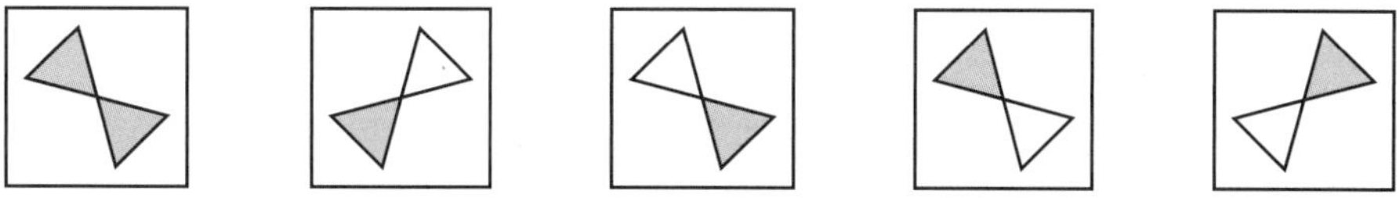

a b c d e

37

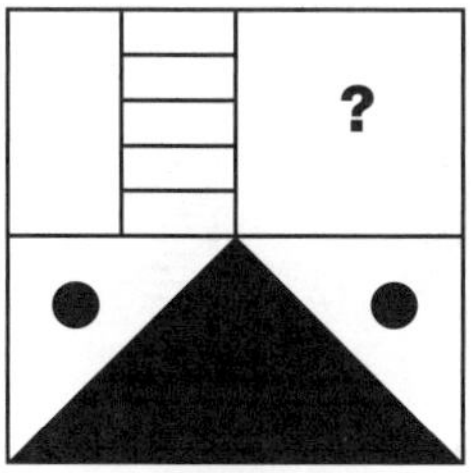

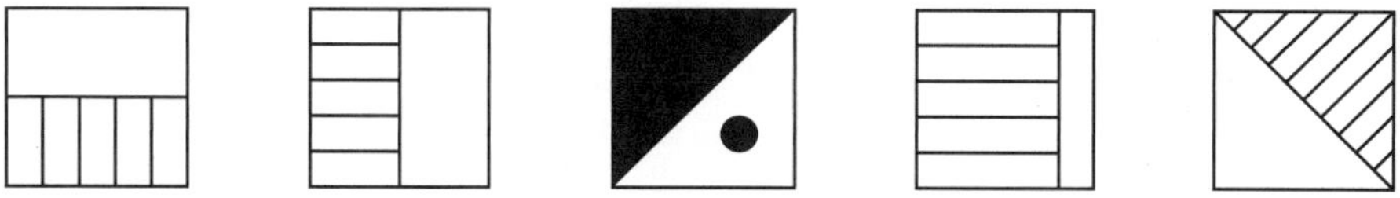

a b c d e

38

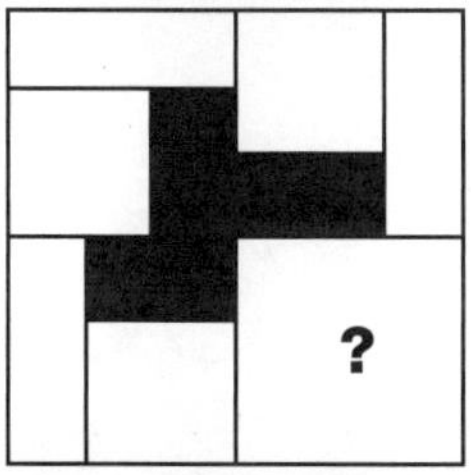

a b c d e

39

a b c d e

40

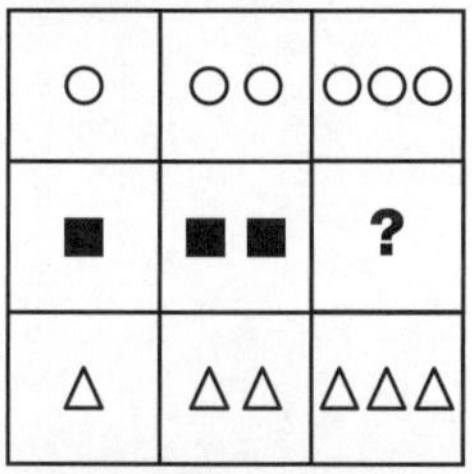

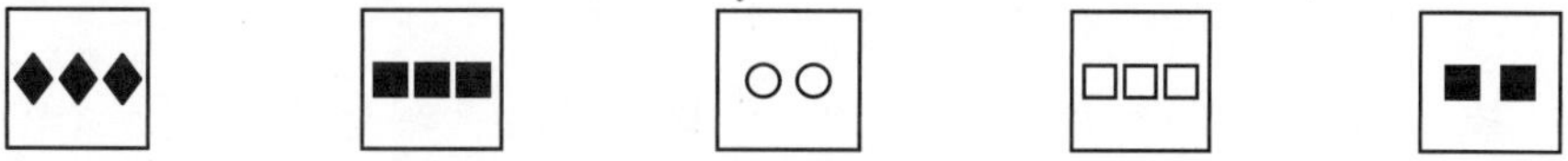

a b c d e

41

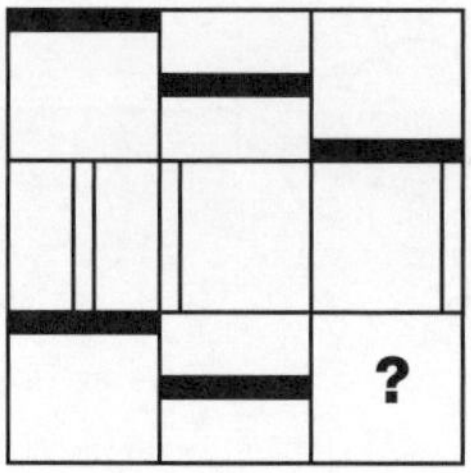

a b c d e

42

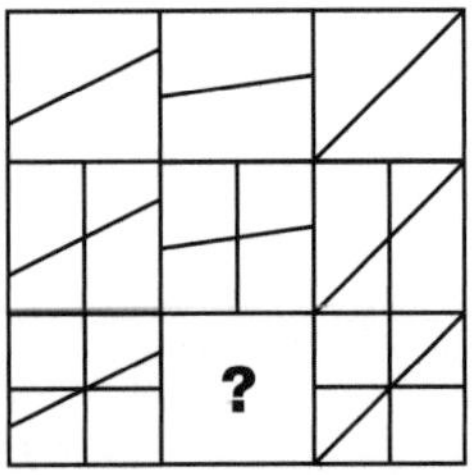

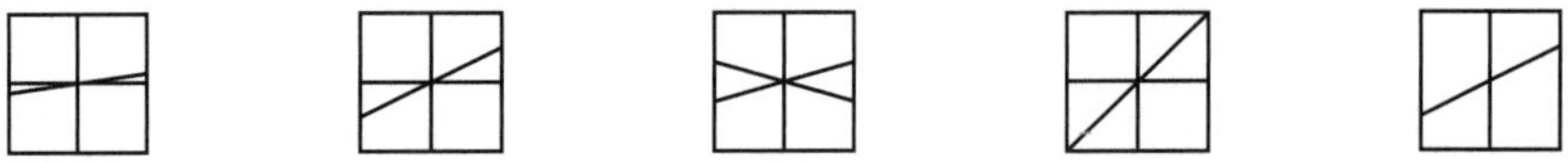

a **b** **c** **d** **e**

Which code matches the shape or pattern given at the end of each line?
Circle the letter.

Example

AX AY BZ CY BX ?

a BZ **b** AZ **c** CX **d** BY **e** CZ

43

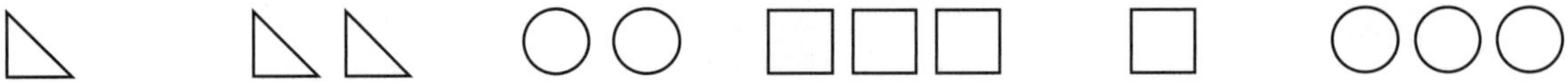

BK BJ AJ CL CK ?

a BL **b** AL **c** CJ **d** CK **e** BK

44

HT FT GR GS FR ?

a HS **b** FT **c** FS **d** HR **e** GT

45

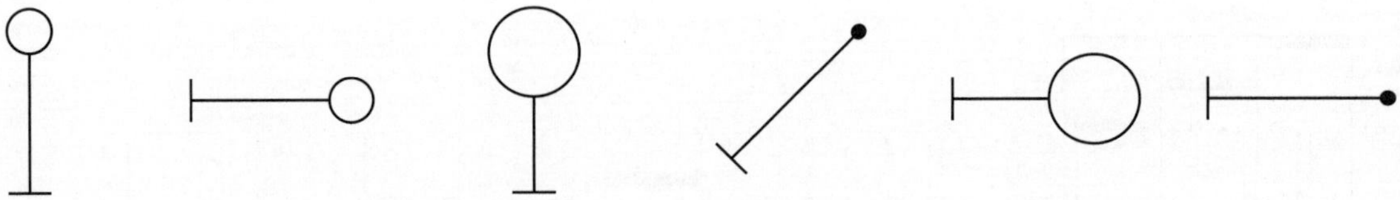

ZQ XQ ZR YP XR ?

a YR **b** ZP **c** XQ **d** YQ **e** XP

46 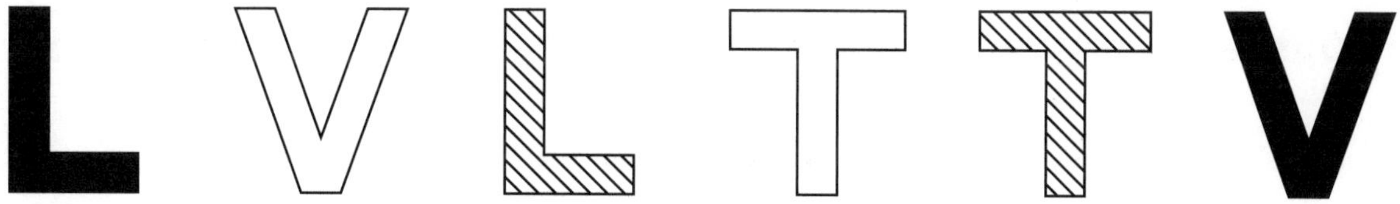

GB HC IB HA IA ?

a IC **b** HC **c** HB **d** GC **e** GA

47 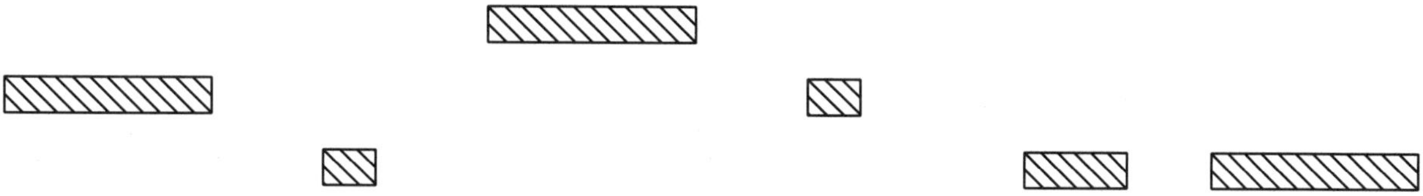

EO FM DO EM FN ?

a FO **b** DM **c** EN **d** DN **e** EO

48 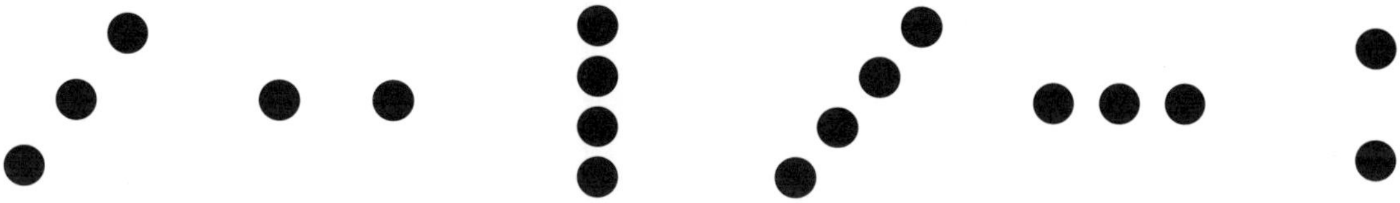

VN UL WM WN VL ?

a UN **b** WL **c** VM **d** WM **e** UM

Now go to the Progress Chart to record your score! **Total** ◯ **48**

Progress Chart Non-verbal Reasoning Assessment Papers 8–9 years

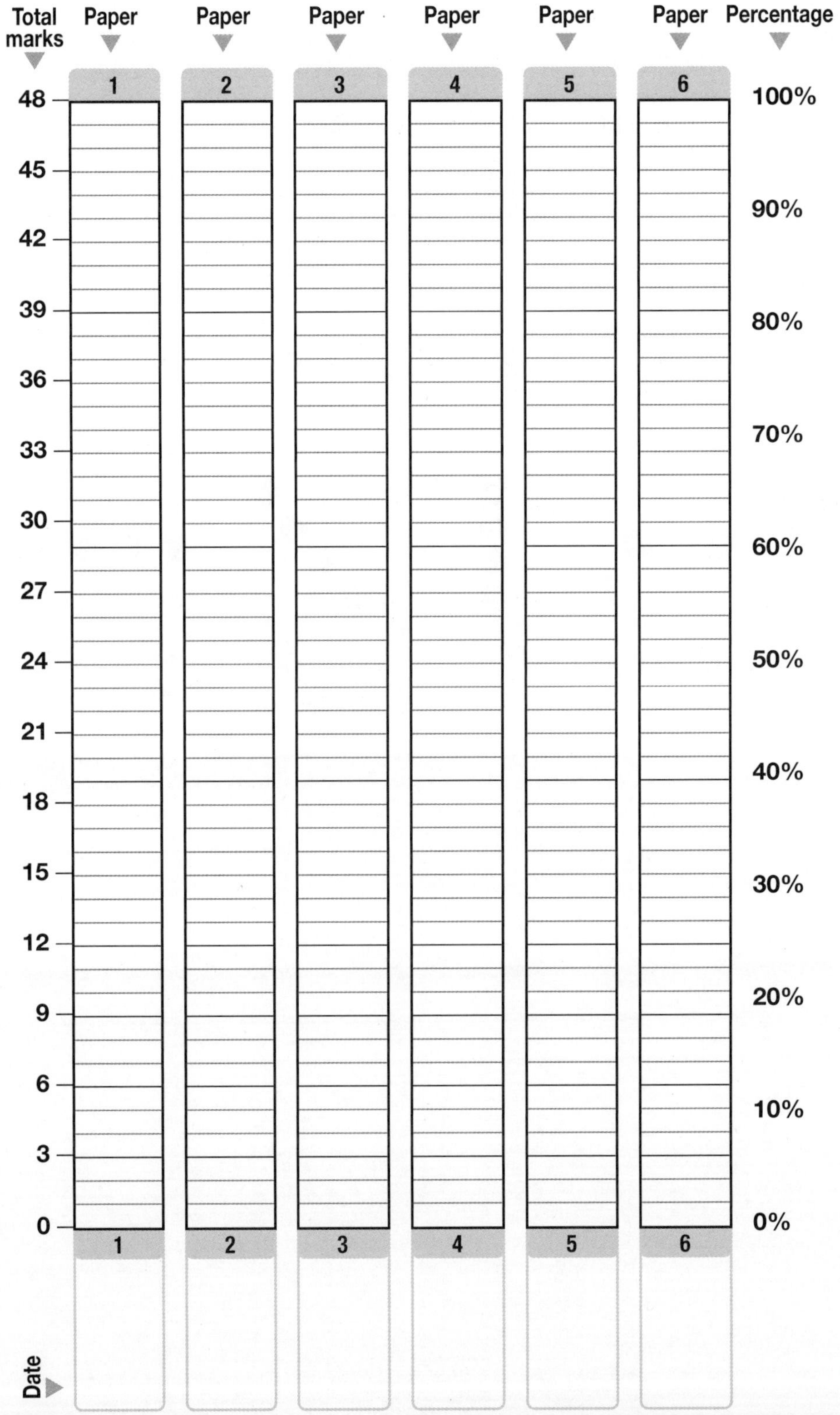

When you've finished the book use the Next Steps Planner